"I CAN DO THIS; I CAN DIE"

Sharon Parenteau

Note for Librarians: A cataloguing record for this book is available from Library and Archives Canada at www.collectionscanada.ca/amicus/index-e.html
ISBN 1-4251-0704-4

PUBLISHING™

Offices in Canada, USA, Ireland and UK

Book sales for North America and international:
Trafford Publishing, 6E–2333 Government St.,
Victoria, BC V8T 4P4 CANADA
phone 250 383 6864 (toll-free 1 888 232 4444)
fax 250 383 6804; email to orders@trafford.com
Book sales in Europe:
Trafford Publishing (UK) Limited, 9 Park End Street, 2nd Floor
Oxford, UK OX1 1HH UNITED KINGDOM
phone +44 (0)1865 722 113 (local rate 0845 230 9601)
facsimile +44 (0)1865 722 868; info.uk@trafford.com
Order online at:
trafford.com/06-2462

10 9 8 7 6 5 4 3 2

STONEWALL JACKSON AND ALICE before they were married. I still wear the black onyx ring he gave her later that day. Stonewall looks alot like Leonardo Decaprio.

Alice Elizabeth Meyers

Mom & Dad

Sharon and Dad 1956
(Susie was not born yet!)

Sharon and Grandfather
(1952 Cowboys and
Indians!)

Sharon Evonne 11 years old. The house on
Endwell St. The new house on Evelyn St. was
being built.

Sharon and Vanessa 1955
(My most favorite picture of me ever taken. I
look at it and say "THERE I AM!")

v

Mother and father
with Sharon and Cork

Not Susie. Susie had been gone for a
year

Sharon and Cork xmas 1950

Cork and Sharon

Cork and Sharon 1986
(the day after our father died)

Rev. Tuttle

Alice and Manley Sr.

Sharon

Cork

Cottage front porch
Aunt Jan feeding her family

Cottage in Windsor, N.Y.
Sharon at her favorite place.

Grandma in her kitchen on
Endwell St. 1961

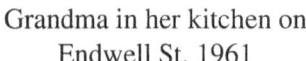

Grandma and Grandpa on the
Boardwalk

1966

Sharon and Grandfather at the worst of my eating disorder out in front of the house he had built in the early 1960's

Nicelee 23

Daughters

Mindette 20

Table of contents

DEDICATION

MY SECOND BOOK was deposited into my brain by way of things astrological. The sun; the stars...and especially the moon, has put me under several spells in order to release such magic! I find myself up in the middle of the night and groping for pen and pad. It is a whole other world. The witching hour! Blue midnight! Stillness, silence, so "loud" it can be maddening.

During my middle of the night wanderings; I search the heavens for my ride to paradise. Surely my space craft is up there somewhere circling and waiting for the declaration to float me off my feet and ascend me! I see lots of things in the night skies; they are not all just stars to me.

As I swim and sit in the sun's light, I feel the feeding. Am I feeding from it or is it feeding from me? Our solar system hurts my eyes............it hurts my skin..................yet the heat goes deep and becomes a part of who I am. If I feed (or it feeds) too long, it does great damage. My body and mind suffer from the feast. After the anguish, comes the sheer glow from within and without. Everything in life follows a pattern. For this we should be grateful.

I dedicate this book to the whole of the universe, as I will soon be a big part of it. I still have so much to learn, but my teachers will then be "the source." Who better to learn about the sun, but from our very own solar system? Where better to rest, but upon a star, and how better to reach the "light" than by way of the moon!

I awoke in the wee hours on June 17th 2003, in a fashion that was entirely new to me. I was lying on my back, and as I opened my eyes, I was completely covered in a moonbeam! Our bedroom window was located in front and directly across from the bed. I gazed out at the man in the moon. The orb seemed to have dropped in the night sky lower than I had ever seen it. He appeared to be looking in at me. The light was dancing across my nightgown and legs, and formed rays of illumination that was filtering up through my toes! Are things really as delightful as they seem, or do they just appear to be because my time to experience them is now limited? I so wanted it to be a shaft of luminosity coming from a spacecraft from another place, time, space, or dimension. "Listen to me" The moon drops by to glow on me and I wish for an alien spacecraft!

It saddens me to have to tell you that I am no longer being "visited." The orbs did not follow me to our new address. I have not seen my doll, Suzie, for over 27 years. The little girl sitting next to my doll on the "mist" floor is still unknown to me. No more implants have entered my body by way of alien hands; nor has anything been taken from me. My daughters are safe and my oldest granddaughter swears, (as I constantly grill her) that she has never been visited or seen an alien, other than on TV.

I am being visited no more…………………..I can't tell you how sad that makes me feel. I was always given the impression that we were somehow connected. Could "they" also be a part of the family of man as we know it? Who are they and where do they come from? Are they real or do they only exist in the minds of men? Can our own conscious power transport us to worlds unknown? Or is their touch real; as real as we know reality to be? I need to find out………….… they have been a part of my life since age seven…. …………..somehow they are tied to us……………..not to all of us………………..and why not to all of us? I am ready to find the answers. I need to find the answers………I feel myself disappearing little by little each day as my soul seeks to possess the truth. Be it tied to God, or just linked in some way; or, if their world has its own god; I want to be a part of both worlds. Will reality rule in my favor or must I choose my own destiny? "Time will only tell....................What is "real" will only tell...................Then I will never tell.................

After the moonbeam visit, I got out of bed, sat at the kitchen table and wrote "Ride a Moonbeam to Heaven." The date was 6-17-03.....the time was 2:00 am.

RIDE A MOONBEAM TO HEAVEN
BY SHARON PARENTEAU

RIDE A MOOMBEAM TO HEAVEN.
    THAT'S WHAT YOU ARE.
FOLLOW IT TO SOME BRIGHT DISTANT STAR.
    NEVER LOOK BACK; YOU'RE IN YOUR MAKER'S HANDS.
    FOLLOW IT TO SOME BRIGHT DISTANT LAND.

RIDE A MOONBEAM TO HEAVEN.
    THAT'S WHO YOU ARE.
IT'S REALLY NOT GOING TO BE VERY FAR.
    NEVER LOOK BACK; FOR YOU'RE IN YOUR MAKER'S HEART.
    WE REALLY WON'T BE THAT FAR APART.

RIDE A MOONBEAM TO HEAVEN.
    THAT'S WHY YOU ARE.
REJOIN WITH YOUR MAKER
    AND STAY IN HIS CARE.
NEVER LOOK BACK; WE'RE NOT HERE ANYMORE.

OUR JOURNEY HAS STARTED TOO; WE'LL MEET AT THE "DOOR!"

RIDE A MOONBEAM TO HEAVEN
AND BASK IN ITS LIGHT……………
LOOK UP AND HANG ON, AND ENJOY YOUR FAST FLIGHT;
IT'S GOING TO BE BETTER THAN FLYING A KITE!
ALL CHILDREN HAVE DONE THIS, AND JUSTIFIABLTY WHY;
IT GOT US ALL READY, TO LIVE, NOT TO DIE.

LOOK UP AND HANG ON, LIKE YOU DID AS A KID,
THIS TIME, WITH GOD AS YOUR CAPTIAN…ABOVE AND AMID.
AMID ALL THE TROUBLE AND STRIFE ON THIS EARTH;
YOU'RE GOING TO RISE UP AND TAKE ON A RE-BIRTH!

RIDE A MOONBEAM TO HEAVEN,
BE ONE OF HIS KIND.
YOU'LL NEVER COME BACK; YOU'RE LIKELY TO FIND!
NEVER LOOK BACK, JUST STAY WITH THE FLOW…….
ONCE YOU GET THERE, YOU'LL KNOW WHERE TO GO.
THERE WILL BE PEOPLE WAITING; ALL FACES LOOK FRESH…….
THEY'LL ALL TAKE YOU HOME TO YOUR NEW, FANCY ADDRESS.

LOOK UP AND HANG ON; HANG ON TO THE HAND……..

IT'S GOD'S THAT WILL LEAD YOU TO THE PROMISE LAND.

WE'LL SEE YOU AGAIN; WHAT WILL SEEM LIKE TOMORROW......

IN HEAVEN THERE'S NO SUCH THING AS SORROW.

RIDE A MOONBEAM TO HEAVEN.

REJOIN WITH YOUR MAKER;

IT SOUNDS SO GOOD....DO I HAVE ANY TAKERS?

WE'LL MEET BY AND BY ON THE RIVER BANK.......

IT'S GOD AND GOD ONLY, WHICH WE HAVE TO THANK.

HUMANITY...RAISE YOUR VOICE AND YOUR HEARTS UPON HIGH......

YOU'RE GOING TO RE-LIVE; ....YOU REALLY WON'T DIE!

TRUST IN THE LORD AND HIS KINDNESS YOU'LL FIND........

PUT YOUR HAND IN HIS HAND AND STAY BY HIS SIDE.

HUMANITY...BE AT THE GATE, WHEN WE ALL GET THERE TOO..........

YOU'LL BE OUR GREAT TOUR GUIDE; WE'LL ALL LOOK FOR YOU!

HAVE A HOT MEAL WAITING, PREPARED BY YOUR MAID........

WE'LL ALL SIT AROUND AND LET LAUGHTER CASCADE.

WE'LL HAVE SO MUCH FUN; WE'LL ALL BE SO MERRY..........

WE'LL ALL WONDER WHY WE WANTED TO TARRY.

WE'LL WALK AND WE'LL SWIM IN THE SPLENDOR OF HIS LAND.......

WE'LL GET THERE, HUMANITY, JUST PUT YOUR HAND IN HIS HAND.

RIDE A MOONBEAM TO HEAVEN!

IT'S NO LONGER A STRING…………..

GRAB HOLD OF HIS HAND…………….

FOR HE IS OUR KING!

ACKNOWLEDGEMENTS

THE PAST AND the future have always intrigued me. The present has always eluded me. In relation to reality; there is no present. The present is one second minus another second; thus non-existing. So I find it quite normal to dwell in the past and the future.

THANK YOU to all who have read my first book! In my mind.............I have stood in a Grande Auditorium (on a stage) above masses and masses of civilization as they stand and chant "author, author." I am very gracious as I giggle and bow at the waist; a thank you to all. It is one of the favorite things I like to do in my mind.

I can never stop writing now that I have begun. I am the word and the words are mine. I need not air nor drink anymore; I just need language. Every time I think how I, you, or anyone who writes down a sentence, paragraph, article, or a book, that it's the very first time those particular words were grouped together to convey a message, thought, or idea for the first time in the entire universe. I am in awe. No two people have ever written the same book word for word. Each is an original, living composition leaving the mind of a living creature to live forever on pages. I am in awe.

If you enter a bookstore or a library; you are immediately silent and humbled. The energy those books give off is a powerful collection of thought. Many people find studying in a bookstore or library helps them absorb the knowledge they seek. No doubt it is fed to them from the thought energy exploding from each and every molecule in the room. Jesus, as a child, was found studying at the temple where the books of knowledge were stored. The fact that each and every one of us can enter a "temple of knowledge" on any given day and be transported back in time or ahead to the future leaves us in little separation from the year 12 ad.

When man burns men's thoughts in the form of books, the torturous cries can be heard throughout the cosmos. No greater crime against man could be committed. As the thoughts contain energy, so they also contain life. I cannot even bring myself to discard a wet, moldy, blackened, smelly hard or paper back book. I have tried several times and it always ends up back in a box of possessions to be kept. I need not hear the screams...........as my soul has heard enough.

This is my wish for you.

What is hidden in the minds of men is our righthood to passage. We must listen to all of it. It takes two to be one. Good and evil, ying and yang, heaven and earth, and the life and death process. For without the evil, the yang, the earth and death; how can we truly open our hearts to the good, the ying, the heavens, and life. We are all made with balance in mind. Balance is the ultimate truth for existence. . As much as we are "together;" as much as our capacity to love overflows, we are each on our own separate journey. Accept the fact that you are a separate spark of light that must travel alone. ------Stay in the moment- and you will get where you want to go. The past holds knowledge and the future is your playground. Study all the dimensions; each has a door that will lead you home. Choose your route and begin to travel. Watch for your guides along the way. They are waving and screaming out to help you. Most of all, enjoy and learn from everything. Let no experience go by unnoticed. You will simply be delaying the inevitable. Peace and joy to all, as you travel.

PREFACE

THE GOODNESS OF people.................the power of love...............and the magic of giving, seems to be our greatest assets. To care enough to teach by example............... To give freely without expectation, and to be rewarded for good deeds. The circle is complete and never broken. The circle will survive long after we are all gone..........there will be giving up to get............... until the end of time!...............

PROLOGUE

I HAD A DREAM recently where I was swimming in beautiful blue water. The sun was shining and there were ripples on the surface. It was very lovely. I was all alone and I could feel the coolness of the water as it passed over my skin. I was floating, not swimming, and not standing either. All of a sudden, my skin began to burn as if chemicals had been poured over me. I got out of the water and began to peel off my clothes. I walked up to the house that was situated in front of the body of water. I knocked on the door and a grouchy old woman answered. "Can I come in and take a shower?" I asked, as I tried to cover myself the best I could. "I was swimming in that water and it began to burn my skin." I said. "You're stupid, she said, that water is radioactive!" "But it looks so beautiful; how can it be dangerous?" I asked, as my skin continued to be on fire. "Can't you see those electrical towers right there; that's where it's coming from!" she said. No.........I couldn't come in, but she gave me a thin nylon cover-up because I was without clothes.

I decided to go to my dead grandparent's house (where I lived years ago.) It had been sold after my grandfather died, (but in the dream, I had heard it was for sale again.) I was going to break in and take a shower; while the whole time I knew in my head I was doomed and full of radiation. When I got to the house, there was a little girl standing across the street. I waved her over to me. As she

got closer, I saw that she looked like I did around age six or seven. I smiled. I told her I had come home to take a shower because I had accidentally become radioactive. We both peered through the front window of the house and saw there was still furniture there. We saw no movement inside, so I tried the door. It was locked. My skin was still burning and I asked the little girl what I should do. She said she didn't know what I should do. I was feeling very uncovered at the time. We both sat down on the top step of the porch; she on one end and me at the other. We slightly faced each other, but we were not talking. I just kept trying to make the small piece of cloth cover me. All of a sudden, a middle-aged lady opened the front door of the house. She looked at me and smiled. " You used to live here, didn't you?" She asked. "Yes I did! I answered. She smiled and turned and walked back through the door and closed it. I looked at the little girl still sitting on the top step next to me. My skin was no longer burning and I was dressed once again. Nelson, my husband, pulled up in a van out front and waved me to come to him. 'Oh, that's my husband; do you have somewhere to go, or, do you want to come with us?" I asked her. "I don't have anyplace to go, but I can't come with you, either." She answered. I ran to the van and hopped in the front seat. As we pulled away, I looked back and waved goodbye to the little girl sitting on the porch. Then I woke up. That whole day I had a hard time keeping my mind on the present. I played the dream over and over and over again in my mind. I felt sorry for the little girl left behind. "What was she waiting for.............................
I Think I understand the dream much better now...................I
think she is waiting for me...

THE LITTLE GIRL WAITS ON HER FRONT PORCH STEPS.......

WAITING FOR THE TIME, OR HER RIDE PERHAPS.

SHE SITS ALONE JUST PLAYING WITH HER HANDS..........

SO FAR HER LIFE HAS FEW DEMANDS.

SHE LOOKS UP AND DOWN HER LONELY STREET............

WHERE IS THE "GROWN-UP" SHE WAITS TO MEET?

NO ONE CAN SEE, HER SITTING THERE..............

IT'S ALMOST TOO MUCH FOR HER TO BEAR.

CARS AND TRUCKS AND EVEN A VAN...........
.

PASS BY HER AS IF SHE HASN'T ANY PLANS.

ONCE A LADY STOPPED BY AND SAT AT HER SIDE.............

SHE EVEN ASKED HER IF SHE WANTED A RIDE.

THE LITTLE GIRL KNEW IT WAS NOT TIME TO GO………….

NO MATTER HOW BADLY SHE WANTED IT SO.

THE LADY RAN OFF AND JUMPED IN A VAN……….

ONLY GLANCING BACK ONCE AND WAVING A HAND.

THE LITTLE GIRL WATCHED THE LADY DISAP-PEAR………..

THE LADY IS IN TROUBLE NOW; THE LITTLE GIRL DID HEAR.

THE LITTLE GIRL WAITS ON HER FRONT PORCH STEPS…………

THE LADY WILL COME BACK THE HARDER IT GETS.

IT'S EASIER FOR TWO THAN IT IS FOR JUST ONE……………

TO RISE AND TO FLY AND TO PASS BY THE SUN.

THE LADY WILL LIE; GOING IN AND OUT OF SLEEP…………..

UNTIL HER FIGHT FOR PRESENCE IS TOO HARD TO KEEP.

THE LITTLE GIRL WAITS ON HER FRONT PORCH STEPS……….

IT WON'T BE MUCH LONGER, THE LITTLE GIRL BETS.

SHE STANDS AND LOOKS UP AND DOWN THE LONELY LANE…………..

FROM A DISTANCE SHE SEES A LADY; SHE TRIES PATIENTLY NOT TO STRAIN.

HOW LONG DID SHE SIT THERE, WAITING TO GO HOME……………..

HER ARMS AND LEGS AND BODY FEEL ONE WITH THE STONE.

THE LADY DRAWS NEAR TO THE OLD FRONT PORCH, SHE GUARDS…………

WHO WAITS WITHIN THE HOUSE CONTENTS, TO GIVE THEM THEIR REGARDS?

THE LITTLE GIRL HAS SHORTS ON, AND A DIRTY TEE SHIRT TOO……..

THE LADY COMING DOWN THE STREET HAS ON CLOTHES THAT GLOW; SHE SHINES AS IF ANEW!

THE LITTLE GIRL SEES A SMILE, AND THE LADY SEES ONE TOO……..………

IT SEEMS AS NEITHER ONE OF THEM, CAN REMEMBER BEING BLUE.

THEY STAND FACE TO FACE IN LOVE; EACH TAKING THE OTHERS' HANDS……………..

THEY KNOW THEY'LL BE TOGETHER IN THE SPLEN-DOR OF ALL LANDS.

THE LITTLE GIRL WEARS SHORTS, AND THE LADY WEARS A GOWN…………..

THEY WILL ALWAYS BE TWO PEOPLE, THOUGH EACH OTHER THEY HAVE FOUND.

IT TAKES TWO PEOPLE TO REACH THE HIGHEST STATE…………….

BOTH OF THEM ARE READY; NEITHER ONE CAN HARD-LY WAIT.

THE WORD COMES DOWN AND THEN A HAND……………

LIKE NONE THEY'VE EVER SEEN.

THEY ARE PULLED UP THROUGH A TUNNEL TOWARD A WHITE, WHITE

 RAINBOW BEAM.

HAND IN HAND THEY TRAVEL; NEVER MORE TO BE APART………

THEY EACH HAVE PAID THE PRICE; THEY DESERVE A BRAND NEW START!

THEY HAVE SO MUCH TO TALK ABOUT, SINCE THEY PARTED WAYS………

HOW COULD THIS HAVE BEEN TIME "IN" TIME, TURNED TO SO MANY DAYS?

IT TAKES TWO PEOPLE NOW, TO REACH THE HIGHEST STATE..........

TOGETHER FOREVER NOW, THEY NEED NOT HESI-TATE.

INTRODUCTION....... To cancer

I WANT TO HELP people get through whatever their gift might be. Remember all those Christmas mornings and birthdays when you are handed a gift. Dread might grab hold for a second then you buck up and remove the covering. Trepidation accompanies gifts. Opening the box is the next step. Controlling your face is the next and then comes the words. After the thank you and the kiss, you can relax and breathe normally again. But alas, there is always another gift....there always will be another gift until the end of time. If you can't change things, then it would behoove you to go for it! Does it make sense to you? Find the good that comes from everything. I never would have begun to write without my gift. I can't imagine my life without my books. They have nurtured and comforted me. The words inside have nurtured and comforted my family and friends. I love it here so much now; but I also want to progress forward, faster than the speed of sound! I hope I will inspire you to accept and embrace your life. Laugh and the world laughs with you; cry and you cry alone. Oh so true. Here are some tools to do just that. I am happier than I have ever been in my whole life. I am looking forward to whatever each new day might bring! I am ready! I am willing! I am able!

1

THE TRUTH WILL SET YOU FREE

OUR OLDEST DAUGHTER is a registered nurse. She didn't attend college until

She was 28. She was on the dean's list every semester, and graduated with honors.

During this time, I received my diagnosis. We love you, Nicelee, and are very proud!

She was my lifeline to the medical world of knowledge, and I grilled her constantly.

"Have you found out anything at all about this Cutaneous T-Cell Lymphoma?" I asked

her over the phone.

"Mom, I told you, it's a rare form of cancer and information is limited" She answered. "Did you go to the college library and check?" I asked.

"Mom, I've even checked all the physician textbooks; it's the same small paragraph in all of them." She said.

"Nicelee, I want to know how I got this. My oncologist said a virus; A NASTY LITTLE BUG entered my body through a cut; probably on my hand. I want to know what kind of virus, can't you find out, somehow?" I pleaded.

She had already accessed her computer and brought me piles of articles from other lymphoma patients. But none were from T-cell patients.

"Mom, I'll keep trying, you know I will, but there's just not much out there. I thanked her again.

The phone rang and my daughter was on the other end.

"Hi Mom, how are you doing?"

"Ok, I guess, how's school?"

"Hard, but fun." She answered.

"Did you find out anything new?" I asked her. Silence filled the airwaves.

"Nicelee? Are you there?"

"Yes Mom, I'm here."

"Well?" I asked.

"Yes, I found something else." She answered.

"Really, what is it?" (the phone call was beginning to perk me up.)

"You're not going to like it, Mom." She said. "I don't think I should tell you, anyway, I'm not even sure if it pertains to you." She said.

"That doesn't make any sense Nicelee!" I said. "You're not sure!'

"It's just a word that keeps popping up in the few things I could find

about Cutaneous T-Cell Lymphoma." She said.

"Well, what's the word?" I asked.

"Mom, I really don't think you're going to want to know this!" she said. I know you!"

"Just tell me!" I pleaded.

"Feces," she said.

"Feces! What kind of Feces!" I hollered.

"Just the usual kind, Mom, you know, shit."

"But who's," I asked.

"Anybody's, she said.

"What else, Nicelee?" I asked.

"Nothing, Mom, it's just that there's a micro-organism in feces that can cause viruses in humans. Your immune system was compromised due to stress, and it couldn't fight off the virus any longer. The virus turned your abnormal cells into cancer cells before your immune system could kill them. This happens to everyone, but your immune system couldn't keep up with your fast multiplying abnormal cells that eventually turned cancerous, and your body lost the fight. Your immune system went into overload. Now it is impossible for it to kill the cancer cells that have accumulated in your body, so they keep multiplying." She said.

"Wow, I'm dying because of poop?

How did I get it, Nicelee?" I asked. "Mom look at your past life. Your were always

babysitting . You cleaned motel rooms when you were in high school." She said.

"And I cleaned Grandma and Grandpa's bathroom for years. Do you have any

idea how many diapers I've changed in my life ?" I screeched. "Yes, Mom, I do; it

looks like just one too many. Any of those things could have allowed the virus to enter your body through a simple cut on your finger. It can lay dormant for years, then your immune system weakens, and bam, out comes the virus and takes over."

"I can't believe I'm dying because of poop!" I answered.

2

VALLEY OF THE SHADOW OF DEATH

My brother and I used to play hide and seek, after supper, during the hot summer months. We played in the cemetery across the street from out parsonage. Our parents and grandparents would sometimes watch from their front porch chairs after the dishes were done. Most of the neighborhood children joined in. There wasn't a park or play area in our small town, so the older generation reluctantly let us roam through their dearly departed. However, it was made painfully clear that we must run along the sides of the gravestones, and never, ever step on the 4 by 6 plots of grass in front of the stones.

As the sun began to set and the games became more intense, the natural course was to work our way toward the back of the cemetery. The further back we got, the less careful we were about where we stepped. The only sound was the squeak of the rockers and gliders, making their summer, evening, noises. Occasional laughter would ring from the house fronts where neighbors joined neighbors to inhale the fresh night air that was swiftly descending on our little town.

1-2-3-4-5-6-7-8-9-10 ready or not, here I come! I could fit behind almost any stone I picked out. Backing into the cool granite, I would slide my body down until my bottom touched the ground. I sat as still as I could and tried to take a breath only when absolutely necessary. Some of the younger children would giggle and give themselves away. I was older, so I was seldom found. The humidity in the air was now settling to the ground. This was my only alone; settle down time, after a full day of bike riding, friends, and wading in the creek behind our house. My father was the minister of the only church in town. Sanitaria Springs Methodist in the state of New York.

The names on the front of the gray and pink gravestones meant nothing to me; although I knew I was very close to the dead. I felt safe knowing they were locked in shiny brown boxes and I was way up here. Ally, ally, in free!! I jumped up and ran to the child who was now "it." We were well on our way toward the back of the cemetery. As we all ran to the beat of 1-2-3-4-5-6-7-8-9-10 ready or not, here I come! I would search out my next hiding place. My next stone was much larger and cooler. As I slid halfway down behind it, my shirt would stick momentarily and then drop me to the ground. The dew in the air was now landing on my bare arms and legs. The mist felt like fairy kisses. As I sat quietly, I had time to ponder my day. It had been a good one. They were all good ones back then. As I sat with my head resting on the cool gravestone, I absorbed knowledge as it entered my brain; seeping freely through the stone from someone's ancient past. (Information too profound for a little girl to absorb.) Information I would need in the future, was being stored for later use. As they imparted, I could feel them taking some innocence and youth away from me. Ally, ally in free!!!

The next count would take us to the very last row of headstones. The oldest, biggest, coolest ones. Now we dared run straight across the sacred ground where our ancestors rested. Sunset would be complete soon and this would be our last ally, ally in free for this night. I was more likely to be found now because there was a child behind each last row stone. Who would "it" pick to be "it" for the following evening? As "it" approached the front of each stone, a scream would erupt from our throats. I would sit back, raise my knees and lower my head and wrap my arms around my legs to hide my face. No one could see me now! I was safe and I had been renewed! I had

15

fed from the valley of the shadow of death, and they from me. But I was the one who was free and alive!

My brother and I would run home cool and moist and tired. As we entered our house, we were once again part of the living until the next witching hour arrived.

I have been playing hide and seek all my life. The dead have always been very near. Going into a cemetery and resting my head on the past is no longer necessary; for I, now, am the past. I tried to make myself unavailable until the important people in my life died. Then my seeking began. I was old when I was young, now I am young as I die. All my life I have been either hiding from, or seeking out, those who have meant the most to me. Now I want answers. I want all the answers. So I can do this; so I can die.

3

I BEGIN TO GET MY ANSWERS

L<small>YMPHOMATOID</small> P<small>APULOSIS</small> IS a pre-cancerous condition that may or may not become full-blown cancer. 15 to 30% of LYP patients go on the develop CTCL. Cutanious t-cell lymphoma.

STAGE I of both (as they truly are one in the same) the cancer only affects parts of the skin, which has red, dry, scaly patches but no tumors. The lymph nodes are not larger than normal.

STAGE II Either of the following may be true.
The skin has red, dry, scaly patches, but no tumors. Lymph nodes are larger than normal, but do not contain cancer cells.

STAGE III nearly all the skin is involved. The lymph nodes are either normal or larger than normal, but do not contain cancer cells.

STAGE IV the skin is involved, in addition to either of the following: cancer cells are found in the lymph nodes. Cancer has spread to organs, such as liver, kidney, or lungs.
Cutaneous T-Cell Lymphoma is a rare chronic type of malignancy. In its early stages it usually affects the skin and may stay confined to one area for long periods of time, sometimes for years. The disease is slowly progressive, but unyielding. Patients may live for

many years with localized disease. Eventually the lymph nodes and internal organs become involved. When large numbers of tumors are found in the blood, the condition is called Sezary syndrome. CTCL is difficult to diagnose in its initial stages and several biopsies throughout the body may have to be obtained.

I am stage IV.

SYMPTOMS

Swollen, painless lymph nodes in the armpit, groin, near the collarbone, neck, and back of neck, jaw, or abdomen.

Nausea, vomiting, a feeling of fullness after eating small amounts of food, diarrhea, feeling of constipation, intestinal blockage, mild or severe back pain, pressure on the bladder, ovaries, or uterus.

Within the chest, possibly causing shortness of breath, difficulty breathing, coughing, chest pain, pressure under rib cage, or swelling of face, neck, veins, or arms.

Within the elbow or knee, most noticeable as a lump that may swell and recede. Within the bone marrow causing bone pain and minute fractures. Within the kidneys, headaches, high blood pressure, frequent urination, and frequent nighttime urination.

Within the central nervous system, vision disturbances, dizziness, numbness, memory loss and confusion.

On the skin, manifesting as oozing, scaling, discolored lumps or easy bruising.

Within the liver or spleen, causing aberrations of blood values.

Within the jaw, throat, nose, or upper chest, causing pain, nasal stuffiness, ear pain, hearing loss, ringing in the ears, or difficulty breathing or swallowing.

Relentless itching, ongoing fatigue, night sweats, fever, and aching of affected lymph nodes.

EMOTIONAL STAGES

Physical aspects of fear
Numbness, mental slowness
Detachment
Childlike or nonsensical behavior
Denial
Anger
Sadness
Guilt
Blame
Withdrawal

PROCEDURE-GALLIUM SCAN –REPORT- (technique) following intravenous administration of Gallium citrate, delayed 72 hour image of activity in the body are obtained from head to toes followed by SPECT of chest, abdomen, and pelvis.

FINDINGS: whole body images show abnormal activity in the hila bilaterally minimally extending mediastium. Activity is equal to or more intense than the liver and is consistent with lymphoma. There is also apparent activity in the right infraclavicular region. Activity is slightly more intense than the ribs, but less intense than the liver. There is prominent bilateral breast paraenchymal activity diffusely in a symmetric manner. There is activity in the transverse colon. There is also somewhat prominent mild diffuse gluteus muscle activity which could be stress related. Activity in the knee joints bilaterally and diffusely. Mild nephritis. There is increased activity in the facets of L4-5 and L5-S1. The large bowel is physiologic abnormal. The sigmoid appears tortuous to the right. There is asymmetric sacroiliac joint activity, left greater than right.

There appears to be extensive involvement throughout the whole body.

PROCEDURE-BIOPSEY OBTAINED-skin from right calf excision.

CD30 positive CUTANEOUS T-CELL LYMPHOMA

There is parakeratosis, epidermal hyperplasic with scattered neutrophils, basel layer vacuolization and large atypical cells admixed with inflammatory cell infiltrate of small lymphocytes and neutrophils in the dermis. Also revealed scattered abnormal mitotic figures. Atypical cells strain positive with leukocyte common antigen LCA indicating lymphocytic origin of this tumor. A6 T-CELL MARKER strain shows positive large atypical lymph and scattered reactive lymph.

DIAGNOISIS- CD30 POSITIVE FOR CUTANEOUS T-CELL LYMPHOMA.

This is a letter from my daughter, Nicelee.

DEAR MOM,

HERE IS SOME INFO ON TREATMENTS BEYOND CHEMO. ALSO I PUT IN MY COPY OF AN ARTICLE ON THE POWER OF THE MIND OVER ILLNESS. SO PLEASE............NO MATTER WHAT.........REMEMBER YOU ARE LOVED AND NEEDED BY SO MANY, SO PLEASE.................CONTINUE TO BE BRAVE AND FIGHT. NOT ONLY FOR YOURSELF, BUT FOR US TOO.

LOVE YA,
NICELEE

4

DISMISSED TO DEATH

THERE IS NO highly effective treatment for Cutaneous T-Cell Lymphoma. I was diagnosed in the fourth and final stage of the disease. I tried for years and years to find out what was wrong with me. I was dismissed with a puce paw and a slight wave of the hand. I finally had to give up or go crazy. The rejection was killing me more than the cancer. I knew I'd never have chemo after reading Gildna Radner's book, "It's Always Something." I have more medical records to share with you, but I thought I better move on for now, so you can get that glazed look off your face. I know it is absolutely mind-boggling.

There are those of you out there who say I never tried to get help; to get better; I hope this, and there is more, will convince you I have not been negligent in my search for help. I asked my oncologist for a pill. There are several drugs, even something as simple as an antibiotic, to help with this type of cancer. He utterly refused to even discuss it. He told me CHOP OR NOTHING. AND CHOP IS CHEMO. So I said no thank you. Our insurance company only provides one oncologist in our area. We were already so much in debt from all the tests and operations I had had, that seeking help outside of the insurance plan was not even an option. Nelson and I are still "low income." Every year we get our taxes done, I ask if we have made it to "middle" yet. She is so kind when she says "no,

21

not yet. You're "upper" lower income, but not middle yet. We are the underdogs; we get zapped with the most tax, she said. It would be better if we made less, or of course, more. Unfortunately, I completely understood her.

5

SKELETON

THIS IS AN exercise in humbleness................
    Coping with death and dying.....................
    Bizarre or profound?
    Genius........................?
    These are my words as I apply it. It has helped me and I hope it will help you, too.

Sitting in a chair or lying on a bed; picture yourself dead. You are lying on your back in the vast open desert. Go over and investigate the body. Make sure it is yours. Observe your body for days and then weeks as the clothes dry up from the intense heat and rot away. Look at your discarded body and identify it as yours. Stay and observe until your flesh begins to disintegrate and fall from the bones. When all that is left is your skeleton, stand next to it and claim it as yours. Now begin to rise above your skeleton. Ascend above and move backwards slowly keeping your eyes glued on your skeleton. You still exist. You can still reason. You are aware and alert. You are just without a body. Move up and backwards until your skeleton is just a dot on the sand. Stay there a while and study the dot. When you feel comfortable that the dot is your discarded body, begin to rise higher and higher and farther away. Now you are entering the outer hemisphere. As you look down, you can now see planet earth.

You see the outline of the oceans and the mountains. Now search for the desert. Search for the dot. They are both undetectable. Move even higher and backwards. See our galaxy in its entire splendor. Planet earth is now just a dot. Your skeleton became less than less than less. Realize that in this vast universe; you were but a speck. No longer visible to the human eye. Your body never was more than just the minutest grain of sand in comparison to the whole of everything. Now you are free to travel at will! Go beyond the beyond the beyond! The body is needed no more. It never was. What always counted was your soul. Freedom takes you on the wondrous journey.

REJOICE THAT YOU SIMPLY ARE!!!!!

6

PINE TREES

---

by Sharon Parenteau

I LOOK UP AT the huge pine tree and think of all it does for me.
It cleans the air and smells so good; just think of all we do with
wood.

We never should have messed with plastic; some idiot invented
it when they went spastic.

Hardened chemicals should not come near our bodies; plastic
has turned us into polluted potties!

I wish we could just turn back time and live like they did when
things were sublime.

We have destroyed our great land and the air that we breathe;
there is no such thing as a delightful breeze.

If we sit on our porches and try to think back, all we do is to
cough and to choke and to hack.

They told us progression would be good, we would find, but
please turn back time if you please wouldn't mind.

My body is dying................

My spirit soars high................

I really don't think this is my time to die

I love those old trees of every which kind; they are never very
far away in my mind.

25

I walk in the yard and pull off a small branch; I crumble it well and inhale its fragrance.

I instantly travel to the past, present, future; and I know I won't be here to love and to nurture.

I'm not ready to be placed and put on a shelf; I'll confront God with my plan and tell him myself!

He'll wave me "go on" and then smile and say, "it's your time to try now--have

fun and go play!"

He trusts me and leaves me in complete control; as I head off for Venus and just take a stroll.

But in my jeans pocket, I've stolen a treasure; a pine cone just ready to open its feathers!

Inside I will find many seeds of the pine; I'll drop them here and there as a positive sign.

My husband, my babies, and their babies too, can all come to Venus; we'll all start anew!

Just pine trees and fresh air; no plastic allowed; we'll all live forever on white fluffy clouds.

We can change things for the future, or maybe we can't; whatever life brings, whether here or we're there, we'll all do just fine in our Lords loving care.

So don't worry or fret, what the future might bring; wherever we are, we'll be able to sing.

Raise your voice to God here and raise it there too, for he loves rejoicing as much as you do.

His love and his laugh will sustain us all; he'll always be there to "catch" if we fall.

How many "baby birds" has his mighty hand saved; we've all felt his touch with one foot in the grave.

He's here for our bad...he's here for our good...you should thank him daily...you really should!

He has it planned out, so unburden your mind; go with the flow and stay right in line.

Go step by step behind the person before you, and try not to step on the heel of his shoe.

Carefully move on to the end of the line; go right ahead, you're going to be fine.

Now it's your time to fly and to span; God will be there; put your hand in his hand.

You'll feel the pine trees he created and you found; the seeds simply spilled from his fingertips to the ground.

Marvel with him for your time may be limited; remember the "someone" behind you was timid.

He'll stay in your soul and he will abide, but he's needed by others still caught in the tide.

From the bee to the bunny to the big pine tree............he'll always be there.............for you and for me........................

7

DISHES

My PATERNAL GRANDPARENTS had a cottage on the Susquehanna River in Windsor, New York. By the time I was five years old, we were spending most of our weekends there with my grandparents. Much of my grandfathers' mother's belongings ended up at that cottage.

Under the sink in the kitchen at this cottage was a round tin container with a lid. Tell tales of red and white paint barely clung to this container. It was about twelve inches around and eight inches high. Probably some old timer out there somewhere would be able to look at it and tell me what its original contents were. As I bravely pulled it out off the shelf from behind the curtain on that summer day in 1955, I discovered a little girl's treasure! It now held an array of tiny glass dishes! Some were pale green, but most were white, with little pink flowers. They were not new. Some of the glass was so worn that the shine had turned into a rough surface. There were cups and saucers and plates, and even a tiny teapot! Surely I could serve supper at the White House with such a find! I was five years old, but I put my little arms around that tin and tromped about until I found my grandmother. "Grandma, look, look at what I found!" My funny face must have amused her. She tried to conceal a smile. "Oh, you can't have those!" she said. "Those were your grandfather's mother's toy dishes when she was a little girl." I held the tin tightly

28

and gazed into her eyes. What did I look like at that moment in time? Reluctantly, she said. "Your Grandfather is under the cottage fixing something; you can ask him, but don't be dis............"As I ran, the dishes jiggled around in the tin. I had to slow down! But I also had to find my Grandpa as soon as possible!

The cottage was lifted off the ground and was supported by six-teen old oil barrels, just in case the river rose extra high. You could easily access the under belly of the building by crawling on your hands and knees. All the boys who came to the cottage played under it; the girls avoided it like the plague. It was cool under there and we female species of the Tuttle clan regarded it as a snake pit. Oc-casionally, you would see a snake curled up under it, in the coolness. But one to us meant one hundred and one.

I walked the diameter of the cottage with my back stooped and my chest resting on my find. When I spotted him, I saw he was pretty much in the center of the square building he had made with his own hands. "Granddddddddddpaaaaaaaaaaaaaaa!" I hollered as I peered in at him. "WHAT?" he said. I had startled him and that made him angry. "Hi, Grandpa!" I said. I was hoping he would look my way and see my treasure. He didn't. What do I do now? He had a wrench and was working on a leaky pipe. Hi, was all he said back. How bad did I want to play with these dishes? Bad enough to enter the snake pit? "Grandpa, have you seen any snakes today?" I asked. "Not too many, why?" he answered. "I have something to show you!" I replied. He was still struggling with the pipe and re-mained silent. I took two baby steps toward the side of the cottage. Studying the grass along the edge of it; I searched for the venom vipers with eagle eyes. Not a blade of grass was moving. Two more baby steps and I would be in! Under the cottage there was dusty dirt as the result of years and years of shade. All I had to do was get past that grass. I decided to go for the touchdown! Tucking the tin into my body, I lowered my head to go, but my feet were not moving! Maybe if I talked really loud all the way to my Grandpa, the snakes will all run away, I thought. Before I could chicken out again, I began to "La la la" and sprint toward Grandpa. How much of this whole process he took in; I'm not sure. I reached him and felt instantly safe. A wrench could smash a snake in two! I sat down next to him in the dry, dry dust. It was at least 15 degrees cooler under there. No wonder Grandpa was taking his time. As he glanced over at me; the red and white tin was at his eye level. He looked, and then turned his head back to the pipe. "You shouldn't be in here, you know." He said. I sat still. How much nerve was it going to take for me to make the crouched run back to safety? "Are you almost done, Grandpa?" I asked. "No." He mumbled. How do I get to play with these dishes? I wondered. I lifted the lid and reached in and took out a teacup. I looked at it inside and out, waiting for the next words to come out of his mouth; but he said nothing. With my thumb and first finger I pinched the dust in front of me and deposited it into the tiny cup; he still said nothing. I reached for more dust and ten more dusts until the tea cup was full. Carefully, I removed a saucer from the tin and placed my "cup of tea" on it. I held it up in front of me. I had never seen such little dishes in my whole life! The wonder was left in my head, never to pass by my lips. Had my actions and my face spoken for me? Only time would tell.

The teapot was my favorite! I filled it with dust just to see if it would pour. Could I dare to hope for such joy? It did pour! I laid out all the cups in a row and filled them with dust. I was no longer under the cottage; I was a princess serving her prince afternoon tea. The spell was broken as Grandpa sat up and took one of the cups off the ground. He raised it to his lips and pretended to drink! My heart leapt in my chest! He had had two sons and I was the first girl to come to the family since his only sister died of breast cancer at a very young age. I never felt special and it was made perfectly clear that boys were the chosen favorite. Never once did I feel special because I was the only girl. "Did your Grandmother give you those?" he asked. (What do I say?) "I found them under the kitchen sink!" I said. "How did you know what was in there?" he asked. "I opened it!" I said with a smile. He laughed loud enough to raise the dead. I jumped. He began to empty each cup and place them back into the tin. Replacing the lid, he gently tucked it under his arm and helped guide me out. The sun made us both wince. My skin prickled the instant the sun hit it. We brushed off the dust and I followed him inside the cottage. Grandma pumped the well at the sink until water filled two glasses, and she brought them to the dining room table as Grandpa and I sat down. My legs dangled as his fought to find room. He took a long draw on his glass of water while I sipped mine.

Grandma stood next to the table by him with her arms folded in front of her. I was a good kid, even at five. I knew I was a good kid; really, I didn't dare not be! He had set the tin of dishes on the table right in front of him. He stared at the container for a long time and so did I. Grandma drew him another glass of water. "Nothing like fresh ice cold well water.............never was................. never will be." He said. Grandpa was close to the age I am now as I tell this. He seemed so old to me then, and I seem so young to me now. Which one is correct? He opened the lid and took out the two Shirley Temple glasses. They were a beautiful medium blue color with Shirley's picture painted on them in a raised white fashion. Her name was on the glasses and so was the name of the movie she had starred in. Grandma took them and placed them on the top shelf of the cupboard. "You weren't supposed to get these until you were much older."(My Grandfather finally spoke.) "And they surely were not meant to be played with!" he added. He laughed when he said that as he surveyed the toy dishes. Could he let the past go and let us meld together into the present? Would he let me be the true descendent of Sarah Chandler Tuttle? Could Sharon breath new life back into these tiny old dishes that had been locked away in a tin for so many years? Grandpa finished his water and picked up the tin and I followed him out the side door. I followed in his shadow; as he followed in Sarah's shadow; as we walked to the far right corner of his property. Along the way, he pulled a shovel out from in under the cottage. As he stood on that corner,

31

he looked up at the weeping willow tree someone had planted so many years ago. It provided medium shade as the long slender leaves swayed in the breeze. They produced a sheer, sunlight show onto the ground. He looked up, then down, then up again at the tree. Positioning the shovel point into the earth, he overturned some dirt. After five more shovel's full, he began to chop at the rich soil with the tip of his shovel. Squinting back up into the tree again, he made sure I was going to be shaded. He attempted to hand me the dishes. Pulling back, he began his speech. "You are to take care of these...........at the end of each day, they go back in the tin and back in cottage....................don't break any of them.......... they are very old. If you ever leave them outside all night, they will be taken away from you............. ...." I stood there as if (I imagine Moses did) when God handed down the Ten Commandments to him.

I sat in the fresh turned earth and drank in its coolness; its dampness; its fragrance. That moment is what I hope heaven is like. I was grounded; I was secure; I was loved and I was alive! Had my grandfather just traveled back in time and had the opportunity to see his mother at the age of five? Where is the dirt she played in? We lose surface earth each year to the wind. Sarah has followed her soil to the heavens, as I will soon do.

I added water from the river and made spectacular mud! After a short time, you couldn't tell where I ended and mother earth started. Smearing my arms with mud (to make long, formal gloves) I would serve tea to the royalties many, many times over, in the shade of that old willow tree. Soon the mud would dry and crack and crumble back to the ground. My DNA was transferred! I am now everywhere and everything! I am one with all and now a part of the old willow tree............................

The Gift

When you are given something special
    Though you didn't even ask.
When goodness comes your way
    Then this becomes your task.
You must look until you find a way…that you can show
    That a gift freely given; evermore should grow.
Your gift in turn is given at another time and place.

    You have become the giver and your gift becomes a grace.

Dorothy Egan Spencer   New York State

8

MOTHER EARTH IS REALLY YOUR
MOTHER ENERGY AND MATTER

THE WORLD, THE universe, the hemisphere, and everything in it
are comprised of only two things. ENERGY AND MATTER. The
trees, the rivers, the oceans, dirt, all forms of living breathing things
and all forms of non-living things; everything below the earth and
everything above the earth is made up of only two things. ENERGY
AND MATTER.

From the point of conception to the point of death to the point
of vaporous spirit; we are comprised of only two things...ENERGY
AND MATTER. The food that we eat, the clothes that we wear, the
water that we drink; everything has both energy and matter.

Matter is solid. Anything solid. Energy is composed of several
things. The main energy is the electromagnetic field that surrounds
all and everything. Other forms of energy are wind, the sun's rays,
rain, speech, hearing, seeing, and simply, movement. None of these
energies can happen without a combined reaction. With every action taken, there is a re-action. If everything is comprised of both
energy and matter; where does a common metal street sign get its
energy? It is by action and re-action. If no one is looking at the
street sign, does it really exist? You look at the sign (matter) with
your eyes (energy.) When your vision hits the sign with energy, that

energy bounces off the sign and back into your eyes and then into your brain, up side down. Your brain then turns it right side up and sends the correct image to your thinking mind. Everything you see in this world enters your brain up side down. It then takes energy to transform it back into understandable matter.

It is my contention that if there were no one to see or touch or smell the metal of the sign; it absolutely would not exist! This is my reality. What is yours? What is?............reality? Remember that everything here and beyond is made up of both energy and matter. Can we define reality by using this method? Can we prove that death does not exist by using this method? A dead body at the funeral parlor is now matter. Its own personal energy has left it, but the body still has energy. How? If someone goes there and looks at it or touches the hand, that person is transferring energy to it. Nothing............nothing exists without both energy and matter. Decomposition of matter creates heat and heat is energy. This applies to here and everywhere you could ever go in the whole of creation and beyond. As far as and into the furthest galaxy needs both energy and matter. There IS something surrounding that vacuum and sustaining it. Right now, think of anything and everything that you can come up with. You will find it contains both elements. Remember that looking at or touching or even thinking about anything supplies it with energy. I have a reason for this chapter.

I want you to realize that we are very connected to our environment. We were made to live and survive on this particular planet. Between your eyes is a pituitary gland that acts as your power pack; sometimes called the third eye. All power comes from the sun. That spot, and your eyes must be exposed to bright natural sunlight for at least three hours a day. Years ago, that was just a part of everyone's day. People grew their own food and tended the farm. Thus they were out of doors and in the sun.

The earth contains an electromagnetic field that erupts from the ground. This energy is as a comparison to someone resetting the correct time on a clock. We need our feet and bodies planted directly

35

on planet earth to regulate our inner clock (magnetic energy.) If that is off, then we are not healthy. We no longer walk on the earth. We walk on sidewalks, blacktops, and building floors. If we do venture outdoors, we picnic and sun ourselves on elaborately constructed decking. We are lavishing ourselves right out of life. Can you remember as a child, rolling down a hill and stopping at the bottom to just lie there and feel the rotation of the earth we live on? We need to nourish and align our insides.

Next time you lay in the sun, do it on a towel in the grass. Next time you have a family picnic, do it on a blanket on the ground like people used to. It is vital to your health and existence. Nothing has done more harm to us than the food we eat and the fluid we drink. Your body was designed to exist on a planet with seasons. We are supposed to eat what our planet supplies for us during any given season. Spring yields young, fresh vegetables along with the remaining rooted vegetables you have stored from winter. Summer is when fresh fruits and vegetables abound; consume them freely. Autumn is the time to eat the last of the fresh vegetables and begin to harvest your fields for storage. Winter is the time to eat meat and rooted vegetables and breads made from the whole grains you have stored.

There is a cycle to life. This law cannot be broken. As creatures of this planet, we must harmonize or parish. The water you drink should come from within the earth. A babbling brook purifies itself as it passes over the rocks, creating and consuming oxygen. Our bodies were designed to move. Movement sends oxygenated blood to our muscles. Cancer cannot live...........cancer CAN NOT live in an oxygenated environment.

Cancer thrives on acid. Cancer cannot survive in an alkaline environment. Our current lifestyles are void of oxygen and alkaline. You can alkaline your inner body with fresh fruits and vegetables, pure water, and anything that springs forth from the earth. Our current lifestyles are void of sunlight and exposure to the earth's electromagnetic field. We are all dying. Next time swim in a "live" body of water. Choose the river, a pond, a lake or the ocean and feed your inner and outer self. Your skin will absorb minerals and energy from the living water. They are there for exactly that purpose.

Cancer statistics are now 1+1\2 out of 3 people; who will have some form of cancer in their lifetime. To me that is 1 out of 2; but then again, I'm not a "doctor." We need to get back and get our children back to the good old days. I know I'm a dreamer. That is never going to happen. We've gone too far to go back now. I call us all "damaged goods." It's too sad to think about. It's no longer safe for our children to go outside and play. We are a dead race. A dead world.

I wish my next chapter were a solution to this chapter, but there is no solution. All I can offer is knowledge and encourage you to obtain more on your own. Keep your eyes on the heavens and your heart tuned into God, and do unto others as you would have them do unto you, and I promise you're going to make it Home!

MY MOTHERS

I HAVE TWO CARING MOTHERS; MOTHER EARTH AND MOTHER BIRTH.
BOTH TRIED TO TAKE GOOD CARE OF ME BUT THAT WAS NOT TO BE.
I SELDOM LISTENED TO EITHER; MY EGO WAS SO LARGE...
NOW NEITHER MOTHER HAS A CHANCE TO PLAN A DEFENSE GUARD.
IT'S TOO LATE FOR ME NOW, FOR, AS I LISTENED NOT.
I REALLY REVELED IN BEING A STUPID, BRATTY SNOT.
I'M PAYING NOW FOR MY BOOSTFUL WAYS; NO ONE WAS SMARTER THAN I…………..
NOW BOTH MOTHERS THAT HOLD ME IN THEIR HEARTS, CAN'T HELP ME AS I DIE.

I SHOULD HAVE EATEN MORE BOUNTY, PROVIDED
BY MOTHER EARTH;
   I SHOULD HAVE LISTENED TO THE ADVISE,
FROM DEAR SWEET MOTHER BIRTH.
THEY CARED AND LET ME KNOW SO; I THOUGHT I
WOULD BE HERE…
   TO EAT AND LISTEN LATER; DEATH DID NOT
SEEM SO NEAR.
NO MATTER HOW MANY FRUITS AND VEGETABLES
I NOW EAT DAY TO DAY:
NO MATTER HOW MUCH I LISTEN AND NOW HEAR
WHAT THEY SAY.
   I'VE MADE MY BED AS A CARELESS CHILD;
KNEW ALL THERE WAS TO KNOW……….
NOW I PAY FOR MY INDULGENCES AND NOW I
HAVE TO GO.
   IT'S NOT THAT BAD TO LEAVE NOW; I'M GOING
SOMEPLACE GRAND;
I ONLY WISH MY MOTHERS COULD JOIN ME; WE'D
ENTER HAND IN HAND.
   PROTECTION ON EACH SIDE OF ME; MY GOD
STANDS UP IN FRONT;
I NEED NOT LOOK BACK ANYMORE AND THAT'S
EASY TO CONFRONT.
   I'LL LOOK FOR THE LIGHT, THE RAINBOWS, THE
COLORS AND THE ANGELS.
I HAVE CONFIDENCE THEY'LL BE THERE; I'LL BE
DRESSED IN GOLD DRENCHED BANGLES!
   I'LL MEET MY PAST HEREDITY AND JOIN MY
FORMER ANCESTRY.
WE'LL MIX WITH ALL HUMANITY AND FLY TO
PLACES HEAVENLY!

Sharon Parenteau   fall of 2003

9

PLAYER PIANO

OUR PARSONAGE IN Lanesboro, Pa., had a player piano. My mother and I were thrilled about it. I'll never forget the first time we walked through that house and my mother spotted that piano. She let out a squeal like no other I ever heard before, which came from deep within her. She rushed to its side and pulled the two-seated wobbly bench out away from the keys. She sat down right in the middle of the bench. There was no room for another buttocks anywhere. She had definitely planned it that way. This was to be her source of joy for our reign in Lanesboro.

She tickled the ivories to hear the pitch and tone. As long as it played; she thought it was perfect. For the first time in her married life, she did something other than clean the new parsonage the first day we moved in. Inside the piano bench was a treasure trove of music scrolls. She also found a medium size box with more of them, in the hall closet. The scrolls were boxed in very faded maroon, dark green, and black rectangular boxes. Some boxes were barely holding together, but boxed they were just the same. After she read all of her choices, she threaded one onto the piano spool and hooked the metal end onto the catch to begin its roll. At first, she sat all by herself and pumped the foot pedals. The bellows must have had a zillion pin holes resulting from old age, because a lot of the air could be heard rushing right out of the air bags, never reaching the little squares cut out of the aged paper that rang forth the song.

The first day she claimed it as her own. Cork and I sat on each side of her as she pumped and sang from her very soul. All................ day.................long. The words were printed beneath the squares, but most of the songs were hymns and she knew them all! We learned a lot about our mother that day. She wasn't always grumpy, and she loved to sing her heart out! We learned she'd rather sing than holler, so we liked it when she sang. We learned our mother had great talent that she was never able to pursue. That makes me sad for her today. Her voice has passed its prime; sometimes it crackles, but not like a witches, just like a mother who has loved too long. The hymns she hums now have incorporated themselves in her being and will never let go. Her chance to be a star to the world has passed by. My mother has a beautiful singing voice. My mother missed the singing "boat."

Our parsonage in Lanesboro, Pa., had a player piano. My mother and I were thrilled about it. I'll never forget the first time we walked through the house and I spotted that piano. I let out a squeal like no other I'd heard before, come from deep within me. My mother beat me to the bench that day. She beat me to the bench the day we moved in too, but after that, the piano primarily became mine. I had heard all the scrolls the day before as I listened to my mother sing through them all. One caught my attention and would not release itself from the singing cells of my brain. "Don't Fence Me In." It was easy to sing and the tone was common ground, so I could bounce both the piano keys and my voice off the parlor walls.

I never asked if I could touch that piano; I just walked myself right over to it and sat down. Touching this key and that key as lightly as I could; I tested my chances to ever get my hands on this marvelous invention. I opened the bench and searched through the faded boxes as I read each label. "Don't Fence Me In" was in one of the dark green, faded boxes. I found that entirely apropos. I hooked the metal tab to the scroll holder and took my seat. With my right

40

foot only, I pushed on the right bellow, but only the tip of my toes would reach. I soon discovered that wind bellows need much more than toes to produce wind. I shoved the bench so close that my stomach was crushed against the keyboard. My feet now reached the two contraptions that would fill the house and my soul with music. Grabbing with both hands, fingers pointed upward, I grasped the wooden ledge beneath the keyboard. Leaning back, fingers almost turning white, I began to pump my feet up and down. I say my feet; it also involved both legs, as the strain and the pain traveled past my groin muscles to my stomach muscles. This is what I call "feeling the music!" It didn't take long to get all those muscles coordinated and working together. I became "one" with the instrument. I was a specialist in short time! My rewards were spectacular! I didn't start singing until I had run through the leg movements a couple of times. Soon I was whispering the words as the scroll whizzed past my eyes. "Give me land lots of land under starry skies above...... don't fence me in.......let me be by myself in the even'nin breeze; listen to the murmur of the cottonwood trees........don't fence me in. Let me ride through the woods where the west commences; gaze at the moon till I lose my senses; can't stand hobbles and I can't stand fences.....don't fence me in!

I began to belt it out like Della Reese, another one of my dad's favorite singers. We went to a County Fair once with the express purpose to hear and see her in person. The bleachers were full as she began her performance. It was 1958 and she was giving us her all! First it started to sprinkle, then rain, then downpour. People scattered here and there. There was no covering anywhere; nowhere to get out of the rain. Della was also caught in the downpour, but she kept right on singing. My dad stood and cheered her on, as he told the people sitting closest to us. "Don't leave, it's only rain and this is Della Reese!" They glanced his way and sprinted to their cars. My father became angry and Della saw the whole thing. I swear, as God is my witness, my father had tears in his eyes. Besides the four of us, there may have been three other people remaining on the bleachers. My wonderful, beautiful dad rose to his feet as he grabbed at his family to do the same. He cheered her on and we cheered her on. She had come so far to entertain. The other three people rose and cheered. Della sang her heart out for my dad. She had watched the whole event unfold. She finished that song and sang us one more. Dad blubbered and clapped as the rain splattered off his hands and right into my brother's face and mine. If God had not been so busy at that moment, I'm sure the sun would have come out. My father was the sun, the moon, and the stars in the heavens for so many people. His heart broke so easily. She thanked us and bowed and walked down off the stage by way of the side stairs and disappeared. We were not to get to see her closer. Maybe this was better for dad. Maybe she had to remain untouchable. Following that weekend, that Monday, when the school bus dropped us off at home, Della was in our house singing! Cork and I ran in the front door to find Rev. Tuttle in his easy chair, eyes closed, head tilted back and the best smile on his face. He savored every word that spun off that record album. Della was singing to her biggest fan. My brother and I sat down on the floor, legs crossed, on either side of his chair. We closed our eyes and raised up our heads and placed a smile on our faces. The milk and cookies would have to wait for a while today. Della Reese is now on TV on "Touched By An Angel." Her album cover in the 1950's displays a gorgeous curvy woman; perfect hair, perfect makeup, and inside the cover, a perfect voice. If you were born too late, you will never know the Della Reese my father fell in love with. She had the face and voice of an angel. I used to study the album cover for long periods of time to try and discover the secret she held, to hold my father in such thrall. After my father died, her autobiography came out and I read it for my father. Since that rainy day at the fair, I felt like she was part of the family. "The family of man." My father knew exactly what that was. Oh how actions speak louder than words......................We were both free spirits; my father and I. Maybe more like, restless...................Ever yearning for something better........................"Give me land, lots of

42

land under starry skies above……….don't fence me in…………let me gaze at the moon till I lose my senses………..don't fence me in……………………..

My father knew one other person he considered famous. Her name was Imogene Fisher. She was supposedly the ex-wife of Eddie Fisher, before he became famous. My dad went to college with her at Mansfield State Teachers College. She was an art major so I have no idea how he met her. It was probably in the smoky, dreaded cafeteria. He talked about her all the time. My mother was perturbed with him during the "Imogene" phase.

She made my dad a picture of a bright orange gold fish surrounded by blue water with white bubbles erupting from its mouth. It was a small picture, maybe 12 by 16 inches and he studied it as if it were a De Vinci. It was painted very unconventionally. She must have purchased the largest box of crayons available in the 1950's. After sorting every shade of orange, blue, and white she began her masterpiece. With a candle close by and papers removed from the crayons; she held the round end to the lit candle. When it melted sufficiently, she pressed it on the starched canvas, where it left a small indented circle with raised edges. At my young age, I regarded her technique as brilliant! This is how she composed the entire picture covering every last inch of the surface. I liked it myself as a child, but my father marveled and described her talent to anyone who would look and listen.

I ended up in possession of the gold fish masterpiece and still held it when my dad died. At one point, my father left it behind at my grandparents (along with my brother and I) in a cardboard box in the bedroom he slept in, whenever he would resurface. One day my grandmother pulled out the box and began to rummage through it. I arrived by her side just in time for her to move something and reveal a box of condoms. She became very upset and threw the papers back in on top of the discrepancy and shoved the box back into the closet and demanded I follow her.

I snuck back to the spare bedroom later to retrieve the larger than life goldfish; not because it was my father's and not because I liked it that much; I snuck back to get it because I was absolutely sure that someday it would be worth millions! Don't forget who had painted it; the ex-wife of Eddie Fisher! I found it years later in a box in our cellar during the late 1980's. Dust filled the crevices to the point of disguising its true colors. It was the oldest looking gold fish I had ever seen. I ran it under hot water. Not one of my better ideas. Although the heat of the summers and cold of the winters had changed the composition considerably; the hot water sank the ship. The crayon was dried to the point of flaking. I began to panic as the orange, blue, and white flowed down the drain and the canvas collapsed. I stood at my kitchen sink holding the mess and tried to recall hearing Imogene Fisher's name on the news or on "Lifestyles of the Rich and Famous." I couldn't for the life of me, remember hearing that name since the last time my father said it. The dilapidated fish had kind of a burial at sea; if you will. Another chapter in my father's life had closed with me along for the ride. My father is gone from me for now. He is not coming along on my "cancer ride" with me, but maybe he is. Everything seems funnier to me now, and I need that so badly. If I reach the point that my father did, where nothing seemed funny, I want to get my angel wings and rise up to meet him.

At the moment of insight, there is an "AHA' that opens up new possibilities. At the moment the Buddha was enlightened, there was no further reason for any form of violence or suffering among humankind. Buddha saw that suffering and evil are rooted in a mistake about how life works. He saw that the endless struggle to achieve pleasure and avoid pain would never end as long as we were attached to our ego needs. The ego's selfishness and insecurity would never heal themselves; there would always be another battle to fight.

This insight came to Gautama under the Bodhi Tree, just as it came to Jesus in the desert when he struggled with Satan. The fact that the mass of humanity still dwells in ignorance; giving rise to all kinds of suffering, goes back to levels of awareness. In the domain of the mind there is both freedom and attachment; we make the choice which to attune to. Each person sets his own boundaries and breaks through them when the evolutionary impulse is felt.

We've all met people whose problems are completely unnecessary, yet they lack the insight to find the solution. Try to give them this insight; hand it to them on a platter, and still they won't take it. INSIGHT AND INSPIRATION MUST BE SOUGHT AND THEN ALLOWED TO DAWN. As our spiritual masters indicate, this is the kind of knowledge you must tune in to. Inspiration teaches us that transformation must begin with trust that a higher intelligence exists and knows how to contact us.

DEEPOK CHOPRA

10

AS LIFE GOES ON: DISHES

SEVERAL YEARS AFTER my grandparents sold the cottage, my grandfather approached me (during a visit at his house) with the red and white tin container that held his mother's toy dishes. He seemed to float toward me with a big smile on his face. I smiled as I eyed the tin. "Look what I found up in the attic!" He said, as he handed me the container. "The play dishes from the cottage!" I proclaimed. "Go ahead, open it up!" He said. I sat down at the kitchen table and put the can down. I knew he had already inspected the contents because the lid came off so easily. My tired, disappointed in general, older heart and my older eyes and my older everything saw a small pile of dirty, dusty, and cracked old dishes. I lifted out the first piece that my hand laid on; no longer picking and choosing. "Boy, are these dirty!" I said. "I bet they'll never come clean; especially the cracks!" I carelessly moved some of the dishes to the side and revealed a bone-dry layer of cottage dirt resting on the bottom. "Eeeoou...., what happened to these?" I said. Grandpa's smile quickly was turning to a frown. "I thought you might want to take these home for the girls to play with." He answered. My girls were then 12 and 9 years old. We just purchased them the latest in new technology; an Atari. They were glued to the TV set. "I don't think they'll play with then, Grandpa." I said. "Well, you go ahead and take them home; they were yours when you were little." He answered. "But Grandpa, they were your Mother's, don't you want to keep them?" (They were in such bad condition; they couldn't even be displayed on a shelf. (Or so I thought at the time) "Well, don't YOU want them?" He snapped back. "Don't YOU want them?" I answered back sharply. He was visibly becoming upset, so I said if he was really sure he didn't want them, then of course, I want them. I had said the right thing for the millionth time in my life. I hesitate to tell you the rest of the story for you will judge me, but no one has judged me more severely than myself. Please be kind as I tell you the rest. I took the dishes home and never opened the tin again for years. I never showed them to my daughters or told them the story of how they originally came into my possession. I never told them that they had a Great, Great Grandmother who was once a little girl who enjoyed playing innocently with toy dishes.

A few years later I put the canister, dishes and all, out on a yard sale table. An enthusiastic shopper snatched them up. Did I know where these came from? She asked me. No, not really, was my response. If I didn't tell her the story, then she would not look at me with disgust. Today as I write, I am reminded of the marketplace on Sunday as Jesus turned all the tables over that were loaded with merchandise. My table was turned that day. I want those dishes back so badly that it physically pains me. I want that day back with my grandfather. I want my dishes and my dirt pile; and I want the sun and the shade from that willow tree, and the water from the river. I was so perfectly happy. I hate blatantly ignorant people. We see in others what we hate most in ourselves. I have been one of "those" people too many times to count. My dead grandfather now knows I sold the dishes at a sale. I probably "gave" them away. I need a lot of forgiveness.......I also have a lot of forgiveness coming to me............ I will behave graciously about both.

FINDING PRAYER WITHIN US

by Paramahansa Yognanda

Whether He replies or not,
    Keep calling him-
Ever calling in the chamber
    Of continuous prayer.
Whether He comes or not,
Believe He is ever approaching
    Nearer to you
With each command of your heart's love.
Whether He answers or not,
    Keep entreating Him.
Even if He makes no reply
    In the way you expect,
Ever know that in some subtle way
    He will respond.
In the darkness of your deepest prayers,
    Know that with you He is playing
Hide and seek.
    And in the midst of His dance of life, disease, and
death,
    If you keep calling Him,
Undepressed by His seeming silence,
    You will receive His answer.

11

KITTENS

Under the porch; in the parsonage in Rome, Pa., someone previously enclosed it and attached a slipshod-hinged door to the side of it. I knew there was scrap lumber in there from exploring it when we first moved there. You could not obtain access to it, as the old pieces of wood filled it completely to the door. One day, while playing outside, I heard the faintest me-ows. I loved kittens more than life itself and here I was hearing several new little voices. I walked around the backyard hunched forward with my ears physically perked on end. Years later on TV, I was to see Sherlock Holmes investigating and he was also walking the same way. Maybe ears work better when you bend forward. The sound was coming from under the porch in the makeshift shed. I opened the door and heard the faint cries a bit louder. They were located in the back, far left corner, under several varieties of different length boards. Running into the house, I approached my mother. "Mommy, I hear kittens under the back porch!" She continued doing what she was doing. "Mommy, did you hear me?" I sweetly said to her. "Yes, Bonnie, I heard you." I waited for a response that obviously wasn't coming my way. "Mommy, shouldn't we get them out of there?" I said as convincingly as I could. "That's where their mother gave birth to them; she will take care of them." That was her answer!!! "I want to see them, Mommy! I said as I could have easily started crying if I wanted to. "Someday they will come out by themselves when their mommy says it's ok. For now, leave them alone." She said as she walked off to finish her work.

I ran back outside and stood at the shed door and listened. The sound was unbearable to me. I took one foot and placed it on the board that lay right in front of me. I bounced on it a little to see if it would support me. I lowered my weight on my other foot on the same board. I was in!!! (Well, I was half way in) I balanced as long as I could on that board and began to search for a spot to move one of my feet to. Ever so gently, I ventured forward. The next board could have easily sent me flying had I not caught myself and backtracked. I stepped to my side and tried another board, but that one was rickety also. Finally, I had to step backwards off the one sturdy board I had found. I needed a new strategy. As young as I was, I knew I could crush the kittens if I just plowed in and over the boards.

I reached in and removed the closest top piece of lumber and set it next to me on the driveway. It was a small short door so all this was done hunched over as I was during the "discovery." The noise of fresh soft kittens fueled me on. One board at a time and soon I would be able to walk in and see my find. I pulled and piled, pulled and piled for what seemed like hours. There were random piles of lumber all around me; there was even more left in the shed. Now I had to make a decision. How bad do I want to get my hands on these fluffy wonders? I took a breather and decided to continue on with my excavation. Soon my young body was aching and it didn't want to bend forward anymore. My mother came out on the back porch and looked over the railing. "Sharon Evonne, what are you doing?" "I want to see the kittens, Mommy! I stood up and defied her to stop me, with just a look. "Your father will be home soon and he has to park in that driveway; what are you going to do about that?" I surveyed the lumber scattered here and there. "I'm going to move it." "And put it where?" She asked. "Over there." I answered. She shook her head and went back in the house. I began to push, kick, and pull the boards out of the driveway. The meowing had stopped. Later, I was to find out that the mother was entering and exiting from the other end of the porch through a small hole.

I had put in a hard days work, so I decided to continue the next morning. Sure enough, the next morning I could hear the delicate sounds of new life. With renewed anticipation, I got on my hands and knees and crawled into the dusty, spider-webbed shed. I began to toss boards out the door sideways past me. I had a pretty good production going when my mother once again came out onto our back porch. "Sharon Evonne!" she hollered. I straightened up and bumped my head on the under side of the porch. "WHAT?" I hollered from my dark cave. "WHAT ARE YOU DOING?" "Mommy, I already told you, I'm going to see the kittens!" "Bonnie, if you keep that up, the mother will move them to someplace else." She said. "Why?" I asked. "Because she will think they are in danger, and that you are out to harm them." "Me?" I answered. "Not you...anybody." I was sure she wouldn't move them. I had been talking to the kittens for two whole days now in my sweetest voice. I had to quit for that day, but if my calculations were correct, I'd be holding fluffy flesh tomorrow.

I opened the door and called out to the kittens. Usually they responded in turn. I coaxed and cooed and finally decided they must all be asleep. Once again, on my hands and knees, I entered their domain. I inched in and oh so gently moved the last few remaining boards that lay between me and one of my "little girl loves." As I turned the corner to where the sounds had been coming from, my face dropped to the floor. NO KITTENS! Kitten fuzz...but no kittens! The mother had moved them! I starred and starred at the floor. The kitten down was mostly gray and white. I picked up a clump of it and raised it to my nose. I could smell the warm cuddly love of a kitten. My heart was broken. I had worked so hard, but it was not to be. I was confused and disappointed. I carried the wad of kitten down into the kitchen to show my mother. She knew from my face that the kittens had been moved. Tears streamed down my face, but I didn't cry out loud. She hugged me and said, "I told you so..." Lessons learned in childhood are not forgotten. I had worked hard and done a good job, but I was not rewarded............... I had worked and done a good job, but I was not rewarded...............

Mom, Dad, Cork, and I piled the scrape lumber to the back of the property and set fire to it. I felt the heat; I smelled the smoke; I heard the crackle of the dry wood as it turned to ashes. I stood mesmerized by the many forms that one single match took on. It smoldered for a couple of days refusing to die and extinguish, once and for all. What had been a haven for new life was now white ashes soon to be blowing through the wind or washed away by the next rain. The kittens had moved on and I never saw even a glimpse of them or the mother around our house. What had I learned those three days as a young child? Lots! Listen to your mother...........Don't fool with Mother Nature.......you can't always have everything you want......................hard work doesn't necessarily mean rewards.............learn to live with a broken heart..........and.......... even wood has a purpose and a life...................and................ even wood fights till the end to survive.....................

THE CAT
by PAUL VALERY

I fall into reverie before this impenetrable animal being.............
In my innocence, I search its admirable muzzle for human qualities.
I am held in its grip by its expression................
Of I-M-P-A-S-S-I-V-E superiority..........
Of power............
And of absence.
What completeness...............
What absolute egotism..........

What sovereign isolation!

Its full potential is ever imminent.

This creature leaves me dreaming of a vast em-pire................

ULTIMATE GOAL

by DEPOK CHOPRA from the book HOW TO KNOW GOD.

I highly recommend it!

To be able to enjoy incredible freedom in the material world.

No more to have to make choices.

The whole universe operates automatically according to the same principles that were once so irrelevant to the struggle of trying to survive.

What is one thing you can do today to grow in spirit?

Stop defining yourself.   Don't accept any thought that begins..."I am this or that." You are not this or that. You are beyond definition, and therefore any attempt to say "I am x" is wrong. You are in passage. You are in the process of re-defining yourself every day. AID THAT PROCESS!!! YOU CANNOT HELP BUT LEAP FORWARD ON THE PATH!!

Depok Chopra

12

VOICES

I HAVE TROUBLE SLEEPING all night long because my body still houses the virus that destroyed my immune system. My body instantly and regularly tries to kill the virus the only way it knows how; with a fever. So consequently, I live my life with flu symptoms continuously. As is with any type of flu, the symptoms get worse at night. As dawn breaks, I begin to feel relaxed and could sleep all morning if given the chance.

One morning, a while back, I woke up to a male voice proclaiming "YOU ARE DYING." Then I said to myself, "Tell me something I don't already know." That's how my day began. A few minutes later, after dozing off again, I heard a male voice say, "ARE YOU READY TO GO, YET?" I was going to work that day, and Nelson usually makes sure I am awake before he leaves. This particular morning, as I opened my eyes, Nelson was standing at the foot of the bed with his back turned to me, as he looked out the window at our wooded front yard. (Am I ready to go, yet?) "Why did you say that?" I snapped at him. "Say what?" he shot back at me. "Why did you ask me if I was ready to go, you can see I'm still in bed!" I answered. "I'm just standing here; I didn't say anything!" I told him some man just asked me if I was ready to go, yet. "It wasn't me." He promised. This was the second time in less than a week, that I heard some man talking right out loud to me. All my life I have heard a man saying my first name to me; out loud, in my head. It is a stern voice, but kind. Recently, my younger daughter, Mindee, told me it was happening to her too.

I went to work that day and pondered the question all day long. Am I ready to go yet? I think I am ready to go until it is smashed in my face like a clown pie. The whip cream tastes bitter and reality sets in. Am I ready to go yet? If I had my druthers, I'd rather stay. However, if the hand of God reaches down, I will grab it without thinking twice. Sometimes we have to say goodbye to now, so we can say hello to what is coming next. I do appreciate the preparation I am receiving. I am contributing also by reading everything I can get my hands on about life, death, and dying. "Something" is also easing the transformation and transportation.

FROM THE GATE OF THE YEAR
by M. Louise Haskins

And I said to the man who stood at the gate of the year;
"Give me light, that I may tread safely into the unknown."
And he replied…………..
"Go out into the darkness and put your hand in the hand of
God."
"That shall be to you better than light and safer than a known
way."
So I went forth; and finding the hand of God, trod gladly into
the night.
And he led me toward the hills and the breaking of the day
in the lone east.
So! Heart! Be still!
What need our little life, our human life, to know if God hath
comprehension?
In all the dizzy strife of things both high and low, God hideth
his intention.

13

GIVE US THIS DAY...................

Y OU WILL REMEMBER Johnny Horton from my first book. He
was the boy who lived on a big farm in the same town where my
father was the Methodist minister. He was also the boy who got
hit by a car on his bicycle. The family liked my father and my father liked the family. The Horton's supplied our family with milk,
meat, vegetables, and chickens the whole time we lived in Rome,
Pennsylvania. This story is not about milk or meat or chickens.
It is about corn on the cob. From my earliest memories, corn on
the cob had been a real passion for my father. No salt; just butter
slathered thick and then down he would chomp. That was not the
best part for my dad; the best part was the noises he would make
as he savored every bite. The noises brought delight to my brother
and I every summer. The more we laughed; the better performance
we received. His eyes would go crazed like a madman. His corn
kernels would begin to fly as butter spread from ear to ear. He
had butter (with corn stuck to it) on his face so my brother and I
felt we had permission to mimic Mr. Corn Eater. The corn off the
cob flew straight out of our mouths due to uncontrollable laughter.
Dad barely lost a drop. Mom laughed in the beginning, but soon
realized there was going to be a real mess when everyone left the
table for her to clean up.

"Alright, alright, alright, that's enough." She'd say every time, as she surveyed the dining room table and surrounding floor. We soon were back to retaining every kernel. Dad was still yumming it up, and so was I, but we settled down for some serious eating.

Dad loved fresh corn on the cob, so my brother and I did too. Every Sunday morning (during the summer months) would yield us bags and bags of it as the congregation entered the church. There was a table in the vestibule where you picked up that weeks bulletin and deposited your weekly veggie contribution. Dad would thank everyone from the pulpit each week for the plentiful bounty.

This one particular fall, after all was harvested and preserved, Rev. Tuttle mentioned to the Horton's that he "sure was going to miss that fresh sweet corn this winter." "My wife freezes it!" Stated Mr. Horton. "It can't be as good as the fresh stuff!" Dad said. "It's better!" Barked the expert farmer. "Oh...really?" Said Rev. Tuttle. "Tell you what, Farmer Horton, Mrs. Horton will cook you all a meal this winter you'll soon not forget; and sweet corn will be on the table!"

Fall turned to winter, and sure enough, we were invited to the Horton's for Friday night supper. We knew the food would be farm fresh and homegrown. Were we really going to be served sweet corn? Was Rev. Tuttle going to go nuts at their dinner table when he ate it? Probably yes...but on a much smaller scale.

We sat down; the four of them and the four of us. Dad blessed the food and he blessed the people. I never closed my eyes when a prayer was being said. I bowed my head and raised my eyes to watch everyone's faces as my dad moved them one more inch closer to heaven with his words. Dad told us to be on our best behavior. Maybe if we played our cards right, we'd be eating sweet corn all winter long! Mashed potatoes were piled high in a bowl. Roast beast lay in slices on a huge platter. Pitchers of ice cold milk dressed the table............and there.............in the center.............rested a huge oval bowl just filled with hot, steamy corn on the cob! It was just so beautiful to look at! So yellow!...........so, so yellow! So, so, so yellow! Why was it so yellow? I thought. We four sat there staring at that yellowness of the corn. Dishes were passed from right to left with Mr. Horton giving up the head of the table to the Reverend. Dad was in full view of everyone. "Rev. Tuttle, help yourself to the corn!" beamed Mr. Horton. "I placed it where everyone could reach it." Said Mrs. Horton. Dad's plate was already piled high with mashed potatoes and gravy, biscuits, and slices of beef. Our glasses were filled to the brim with ice cubes. That night we were introduced to "fresh from the cow" milk over ice. I don't drink it any other way since. It was delicious!

Dad took a large piece of corn from the oval bowl and placed it on his bread plate next to his biscuit. The butter was passed and a large chunk of it was deposited on Dad's plate. It was dark out and the food was hot and the house was warm. I sat next to Johnny and took just a few mashed potatoes and a biscuit; both still an all time favorite of mine. Conversation died down after everyone had filled his or her plates. "Marsha, this beef is wonderful!" Said our Mom. "Thank you so much, Betty! It is from our stock." Chirped Marsha.

Dad was ready to munch into his corn. He had made such a fuss over it that all eyes were on him. As his mouth surrounded the ear and he bit down, his uppers and his lowers betrayed him. Try as he might, those false teeth could not penetrate the golden harvest. Mr. Horton had long since been chomping and smacking his lips and twisting his head in delight. "Reverend, maybe you're going to have to cut that off the cob!" Bellowed our host. Mom wasn't eating her ear; neither was my brother, Corky. "I think I can manage ok." Said Dad. The corn was horrible...; not edible! Dad's face told the whole story. Mr. Horton insisted he either cut the corn off or gnaw on it with his choppers. Dad was in agony. How could he get out of this one? Sweat began to form on his brow as he forged forward with the ear of corn. Mom was looking at him with sympathetic eyes. She tried to direct the conversation off the corn and on to anything else. Nothing was working in favor of my father. He just wanted to get out of there. We made it through dessert; more biscuits with strawberries and ice cream. Somehow Dad managed to get us out of there fast.

Dad was devastated, angry, and hot! "Can you believe it, Betty?" (He started as soon as all four car doors were shut) "They served us cow corn!" "Maybe it wasn't cow corn; maybe it was just old, tough field corn." She answered. "Betty, don't pretend you don't know what cow corn is! Can you believe they were eating that?" Mom tucked us into bed, as Dad followed behind her ranting and raving about cow corn. "Maybe they eat it for the fiber." Cooed our mother. That night left a permanent mark on my life. Oh yeah, and Dad's too. I never let him forget the night he almost puked eating cow corn. To this day, I have to have almost white ears of corn or I won't buy it. I've accused every roadside stand and super market around, that they were trying to sell the public cow corn. "This better not be cow corn or I'm bringing it right back!"

After that dinner with the Horton's, Dad lost his luster for the eating ritual of sweet corn. Years later, I watched him eat a couple of ears at his brother's house. He said yum and butter and corn was all over his mouth, but it was never the same.

I'm not sure why I had to extract this from my memory and put it on paper. Maybe to remember that what we wish for may not be what you really need. We can't have sweet corn in the winter and we can't have everything we want. We can't choose the course of time or the course our lives take. We can only take what we get and enjoy it in the right frame of mind. If there is no such thing as time and space; then why does time keep marching on? Why do we age? Why do we get sick? Philosophers say we choose the life we have and the people we live it with. I hope this is true. That makes us all choosers and all chosen. I chose my Dad and he chose me. We both got lucky!

A LETTER FROM MY DAD IN JUNE OF 1976

Dearest Sis,   (he called me sis)

Have been trying to write. Trying to find a minute. Have been so busy. So when your beautiful card came, I said I'll just stop and write. The Center is doing absolutely fantastic! I initiated eight new people last week. One young man rose instantly to a very high level and I think he will go to cosmic consciousness very fast. I just cannot tell you the extent of my rapture. We are the only organization emphasizing the "spiritual" benefits of transcendental meditation. And the public is taking it with such depth. The American people are looking for the inner reality and I feel we are the answer to that need. Cork has not gotten in touch with me yet, but don't worry, he will. The sense of our mission grows stronger within me all the time and this organization will grow very fast. I don't know if you could work it out or not, but it would be wonderful if you could convince Nelson to come up here and find work. There would be no problem for the summer because of all the resorts. You could live with us and all have your own rooms. By fall, I have the feeling the Center will be going so strong that there will be some kind of work for him to do with us. While all the while, you and I could be forming the society writing the "Grand Dance Of Life!" and all the other things I wish you were here for. Put your creative intelligence to work and you will find a way.

LOVE, LOVE, LOVE,

DAD   "Mulla Elias"

I never "found" a way to get there. By then, my Dad was drinking and my children were small. I "wanted" to be with my Dad, but I wanted my "old" Dad back. He was gone to us for what would end up being forever; at least forever in this realm of reality. Today as I read his letter and see his hand writing, it opens the floodgates of my youth; my wonderful, glorious youth I spent with my "real" Dad. I have relinquished my youth to this outside world, but inside

60

I am still the little girl feeling sorry for my father for one reason or another. The "Center" never did "take off." I died a little each time he failed. Now as I contemplate everything, I realize he never failed at anything. He really wanted to make a change for the better for the whole human race. He was guilty of unrealistic expectations, but without expectations, we might as well lie down and die. He made a huge difference in my life. I learned so much from him. That would please him to know that. That would have been enough for him, but I never told him. I never told him he was enough for me, just the way he was.................When I see him again, I will tell him.............................

MY FATHER
by SHARON PARENTEAU

My father was the king of all that he surveyed.
    He rained down love on everyone; it fell in full cascade.
Beauty was his splendor…he reveled in it so-
    He could find so much of it; everywhere that he did go.
His laughter killed all pain and bad times in everybody's way.
    How come God didn't give him more time to stay and play and pray?
Was he so special and needed in another world beyond?
    That we had to give up our hero-did God find him all that fond?
I see the two of them now, each sitting on a rock..........
    Gazing out over the waters, exchanging laughter and talk.
I hope there's one or two more rocks, or three or four or more…
    My heart aches to sit there; to be included in what's in store.

My personality will change; I'll sit still, be quiet and listen...........

As my two favorite fathers fill me in on what I have been missing.

Soon the "rocks of ages" will all be filled with many of my loved ones.........

I hope this means that our work on earth will be forever done.

The secrets and the knowledge will be ours to go and work on.........

I'm sure there will be lots of time to go and also have fun.

Will we all be needed by others, as this world's turned out to be...

Or can we stay with our fathers and proclaim a revelry?

I want to stay

I want to go

I want so very much

If it were all left up to me, each life I'd like to touch.

But God has his own plans..........

For mine do not count..........

He knows what is best for me as I haven't any doubt.

I hope my two fathers and I, can go forward hand in hand...

Be the "new" three musketeers of the splendid Promised Land.

14

ON DEATH AND DYING

Y EARS AGO I was asked to train a young girl at a place I was working. She was cute and sweet and trying to find her place in life. As the days went by, she began to talk about herself. She had tried several jobs and none were quite what she was searching for.

During that search, she accepted a job at a nursing home facility as a nurse's aid. She thought it was a way to help others and helping others always made her feel good. Minimum wage was all they paid her to care for our elderly. She did several different tasks. Bedpans always needed emptying and scrubbing. Sponge baths were a must only if you had the time to fit them in. She bathed old faces, underarms, penises, and rearends. She lifted women's breasts and laid them to the side as she sponged and toweled. When she tried to talk to the patients, few responded. Most had to be lifted from bed into chairs with wheels attached so they could be pushed to the dining hall for breakfast, lunch, and dinner. Most needed to be tied under their arms and around the chair so they would not fall forward. The purpose of this was to make the patients sociable. Most had to be fed by aids, and most spit the food back out. It wasn't unusual for some to leave the dining hall with the first mouthful trickling down their chin. As each patient was fed, they were wheeled out into the hall to make room for more in the dining room. A second aid was supposed to be watching them, but that was impossible. There was a shortage of workers. There continues to be a shortage of workers. "Not many stay at that job as a nurse's aid." She told me. On a day they were extremely short of help, she was told to wheel six patients to the dining hall for lunch. She was told to feed all six before returning them to their rooms.

She fed two of them and pushed them into the hall to wait. She wheeled two more in and began to feed them at the same time. When she finished, she wheeled them out and pushed in the last two. Out in the hall along with the other patients, Mr. Jones' arms had slipped out of the tie-down that was around his upper body preventing him from falling out of the chair. When she finished feeding the last two and returned to the hall, Mr. Jones was not moving. The tie was around his neck and he was not moving. He had vomited his undigested lunch. She felt like screaming, but she could not upset the other patients. She ran to the nurse's station on that floor. She and three nurses ran to the hall and found Mr. Jones was dead. Had he slipped or had he found his chance to "slip away?"

Terror returned to her voice as she told me the story. She was never accused of anything by anybody but her own self-conscience. The man's family was simply told that he had passed away that day. Why are we keeping our elderly alive way past their departure date? Why? Why can't we let them go to their glory with dignity? Why? What purpose does it serve to force life into a body ready to embrace the future? Why can't we accept death as a part of life; as much as life is? Nature has to take its course. Only the healthiest are supposed to survive to continue the species. Why do we do this to our most precious loved ones? Can we please begin to give life back to nature? We are an intricate part of that nature and we need to follow that course.

AUTHOR UNKNOWN

And the miracle is………………if you can go into your suffering as a meditation……..watching……………to the deep-

64

est roots of it............just through watching..............it disappears. You don't have to do anything more than watching. If you have found authentic cause by your watching............the suffering will disappear.................find the authentic cause of your suffering..............

RETURN TO THE SOURCE
by   DEPOK CHOPRA

There is no observer separate from the observation. Everything around us is the product of who we are. In the highest stage, you no longer project God; you project everything, which is the same as being in the movie, outside the movie, and the movie itself. In unity consciousness, no separation is left. We no longer create God in our image, not even the faintest image of a holy ghost. To equate God with existence seems to strip him of power and majesty and knowledge. But our quantum model tells us otherwise. At the virtual level there is no energy, time, or space. This is the source of everything measurable as energy, time, and space; just as a blank mind is the source of all thoughts. "The oncness becomes all."

When you cross into the quantum zone, space.............time collapses into itself. The tiniest thing in existence merges with the greatest...........point and infinity are equal. The obvious question is "So What?" The process sounds like dying. One must give up the known world. The end of the chase is the ultimate gamble. You don't play for all OR nothing; you play for all AND nothing.

THERE   IS   SOMEONE   WHO   LOOKS   AFTER US................

FROM BEHIND THE CURTAIN………………..

IN TRUTH WE ARE NOT HERE………………
THIS IS OUR SHADOW…………………..

WE………MUST………JOIN…………WHOEV-
ER…………IS………………BEHIND……………THE
……………CURTAIN……………………………

15

MORE MEDICAL RECORDS

I JUST READ THROUGH them and decided they don't matter any-more. So I did some editing. They are the past. They are boring. They are not a part of my reality. I have cancer that could have been eradicated with a pill if discovered sooner. No one helped me. I went to thirteen doctors in fifteen years seeking help. According to the Doctors, I was pre-menopausal the entire time. I give up and I give in. I am ready for the next part of my life.....................

16

"OH, THE PERILS................

I GOT OUT OF bed one morning and was planning a few errands to get accomplished that day. The house was cluttered, and I wanted to get things back in their proper places before I left. I remembered that I needed to use the bathroom, as it had been a few days. I wanted some relief before I left the house. I went into the bathroom and inserted a suppository. As I was about to leave the bathroom, I stopped. If one suppository is good, then two would do an even faster job! (I didn't have a lot of time to waste that morning) I reached into the jar and retrieved one more. Still dressed in my nightgown, I busied myself with tidying the house. Not even one minute later, I sneezed. Out popped a suppository onto the floor! As I stood there pondering the trials of being a human being with bodily functions, I bent over to pick it up. When I did, my body released another sneeze and also the other suppository! Only this one shot clear across the living room and landed on our love seat! I just stood there, one suppository in my hand, and the other on the love seat. This cannot be happening, I thought to myself. I walked over to the love seat and stared at the glycerin bullet! I found out two things about myself that morning. One, my "buck" shot is about level with a love seat, and two, I have a pretty darn good aim!! No more love on that seat.

Gilda Radner said in her book "It's Always Something" that cancer was the most unfunniest thing in the world. Yet if you read her book, you will find page after page of humor; some very similar to my experience. (Really, Mom!)(She farted out a ball of mercury that no one could manage to get picked up out of the carpet.) (Honest, Mom!) (My mom told me I couldn't add the suppository story.) Gilda chose to fight her cancer with chemicals. I decided to make an agreement with "my cancer" to see if we could co-exist in one body. Everyone asks me how I feel; what does it feel like to have cancer? It must be awful. I'll tell you now that it feels like something alive is inside of you; and there is! When it is hungry........I feed it............when it wants to rest............I go lie down.............. I'll admit it..........I'm at its beck and call.

There is a cancer called Tarratoma. (spelling?) In it's tumor you will find teeth, hair, and fingernails! These tumors appear in children and adults; and in both male and female. They are usually found in the stomach, but have also been discovered in the brain. It has absolutely nothing to do with reproduction. All the horror movies in the world cannot compare to the idea of something like this existing. We live in a world where each day in unknown. We can either live in fear or we can embrace each day with enthusiasm and pray for the best.

My oncologist said "There is no magic pill for you." I just sat and stared at him. He said chemo and I said "no thank you." Gilda did all they told her to do, and a couple of years later, after many times of exhilaration and disappointment, she was gone. Her book is witty and informative and I recommend it to everyone. Gilda tried everything, God bless her. Reading her book helped me make the decision to try nothing.

GILDA'S POEM

My body turned a cold back on me, at less than forty-three.
    It started a war
Whatever for

In the middle of the middle of my life.
It raised a black dividing mass
    In my ovaries…alas
And growing fast.
    What was the point………
A childish attempt………..
    To eat me alive and wreck the count. (blood cells)
My spirit strives to hold the fort…………..
    Shaking its fist at each report.
This is a shame.
    Days…………… spending my life in bed on my back in
the middle of the middle of my life.
    I can see roses in front of my hedge………………..
With doctors pinned on their petal ledges………………..
    And nurses too……………..and you and love and "alive"
scribbled not far above…………………………………

I LOVE THIS POEM!

Never grow a wishbone where your backbone should be.

Clementine Paddleford

This is a recreational universe. Your ability to play in it is limited only by how much you can appreciate. The world's greatest saints and masters may simply be enjoying themselves. They have the ability to live in the light while the rest of us cannot.

AUTHOR UNKNOWN

17

HELP FOR ME

M Y GENERAL PRACTITIONER prescribed Zoloft for me because I was not sleeping. Before that, I took Nelson's Lorazipam to ease the panic that often erupted (in the beginning) from my chest without warning. I confessed, and the doctor gave me a prescription of my own. This is the one single thing I will continue to do until the day I die. Without them, I would have been dead a long time ago. I will do anything to not be without those two tiny pills each day. One is for depression and the other is for panic disorder. My general practitioner makes me come in every six months or else he won't renew my medication. He also knows I choose not to get treatment and he treats me like a slightly nutty person. He is from the other side of the world and I find it hard to understand him when he speaks. (Our HMO picks our doctors for us.) If you are a cancer patient, I highly recommend these two medications.

As time went on, I only went to the doctor for refills; I went only to get my medication prescriptions. This particular day, I had worked all day and was extremely hot and tired. After waiting in the waiting room, I was escorted to a room and left there for a while. The nurse came in and tried to hand me a paper dress. "Here, put this on; the doctor will be in soon." "Oh, I'm not getting an exam today; I'm just here to have my meds refilled." "The doctor has to examine you before he can do that; please put on the gown." "No, I said, I don't need a physical. You can charge me for one......I don't care............but I'm not getting undressed so he can tap me on the knee!" She gave me a dirty look and left the room. I sat there and thought of all the times I'd gone to the doctor and did everything they had asked me to do. Those days were gone. I was a broken woman. A horse ridden too hard and put away wet, to fight anymore.

It was forever before the doctor cautiously entered the room. "How are you?" He asked with trepidation. "I'm ok, I just need my pills refilled." I answered. He stood next to me as I sat on the examining table fully dressed in the business suit I had worn to work that day. "And how have you been?" He asked. "Ok, I said, I'm just here to get my prescriptions." His eyes never left mine. Was I going to jump off the table and attack him if he turned his back to me? Boy! Was this fun!!! (How many times had I been in that position, compliment of so many doctors!) "How have you been feeling?" he asked me. "Ok, I said. He carefully reached for his stethoscope and plugged it into his ears. "May I listen to your heart?" he asked, still not taking his eyes off mine. I held right in there with him. My days of intimidation were over. "That's not where the cancer is, but go ahead if you want to." Through my business suit and blouse and bra he pretended to be able to hear it. He gently rested his hand on my wrist and counted. I was pretty sure the cancer wasn't there, either. He brushed my hair aside and looked in one ear. I was beginning to feel like a very dangerous animal because that was how he was treating me. I was beginning to perk up with "the power" I was feeling. I had the doctor shaking in his boots instead of the other way around. I feel bad now for what I put him through, but at the time, I couldn't help myself. When I left, he watched me walk the long hallway back out into the waiting room. I glanced down at the paper he handed me, that he told me to present to the window. Sure enough, I had been charged for an exam. I knew I would be. He also noted that I was a MDP. (moderately difficult patient!) I stared in disbelief that he had noted that. There's a spot already saying that and all the doctor has to do is check it! I looked for a box to mark that every doctor was inadequate, but that was not noted on the sheet. It's not that I didn't try to find out what was wrong with me. I have the proof that I did. I have lost all faith in the medical field. I know many people with cancer have been successfully treated, and I applaud them, but don't look at me with disdain for the decision I have made. I am listening to my body and it is telling me.........PHYSICIAN, HEAL THYSELF!

My oncologist says.........."This is not about the virus any-more...this is about your compromised immune system. The virus already did its deed and is again laying dormant. Your immune system can no longer keep ahead of your abnormal cells that are turning into cancer cells. Your system is running amuck. Without killing a lot of those multiplying cancer cells with chemotherapy, (and that may not even work) Your body can not keep ahead of them with its natural killing devices. There is little we can do for you. We can prolong your life, but we cannot improve it. THERE IS NO MAGIC PILL FOR YOU.............................I say OK.

18

I SMELL SMOKE!

MY BROTHER ASKED me to tell more medical stories, so here's one about my bone marrow extraction. This was done in the Oncologist Department of the hospital. They have a small operating room and Nicelee, (knee-cell') my oldest daughter and I were escorted in. Nicelee was still in medical school, so she was very excited to see a procedure done that she hadn't already seen. Dr. Keith, my Oncologist, did the procedure with an assistant at his side. Also there were two lab technicians ready to test the fluid removed from deep within my hip-back bone. There is a mixture of blood and marrow running through the center of all our bones. The biopsy test had to be performed as soon as possible, after the marrow hit the light of day. Nicelee told me this was going to hurt. The doctor told me this was going to hurt, and the nurses told me this was going to hurt. They numbed the backside of my hip as best as they could as I lay face down on the table; no pillow and do not move. Ok, I can do that. He gave me a long shot that hurt a lot. They can only numb just so deep, past that point; it's bite the bullet with no swig of whiskey. After asking me if I was all right, he continued. My head was deliberately turned toward my daughter and away from the doctor. I did not see, but I heard the sound of the drill! Dr. Keith soon told me it was time to "break" through the bone to reach the marrow. My soon to be nurse, daughter's face, told me the whole story. Her eyes couldn't have opened any wider. The drill bits quest for oil had begun. It hurt. It burned and I could smell smoke! "I smell smoke, guys." I said. Everyone laughed. That was all I needed. Water was flying all over the place as it lubricated the drill bit. I felt and heard the grinding of bone. "Do I hear grinding back there?" I asked. Everyone laughed. It took some time to get to the center of that tootsie roll pop! Dr. Keith hollered, "I'm in!" and the technicians began their performance. There was solution to be mixed and several test tubes waited for their deposit. The drill was equipped with a drill bit that could withdraw the fluid out. After handing the drill to the lab technician, she released some bloody liquid into a test tube containing a clear potion. She shook and shook and held the tube up to the operating light. "There is no marrow in here." She stated. "Try another sample." The oncologist said. She did the test again; still no bone marrow, only blood. "How can that be?" I asked. "Isn't bone supposed to have marrow in it?" no one answered me. The doctor said, "Try it again." Apparently, my bones were void of marrow. "Absolutely no marrow to test, Doctor." The room fell silent, except for me. "Is that good or bad?" I asked. Nicelee's face was still contorted from the sound of the drill and the crunch of my bone. I lay there as everyone looked at each other. I was able to move now, so I rolled over a little on my side that faced the doctor. "What next, Doc?" I asked. "Do you think you can stand another try?" he asked. "Do I have a choice?" I answered. I didn't think that was so funny, but everyone else did. "We will go to the other hip and extract there." He said with great confidence and authority.

Now my visit was running into the next patient's time. So I asked him if he was sure he had time to do this again. He laughed because he thought I was joking again. He numbed, drilled, smoked, sprayed, and extracted all over again. All the time the nurse apologizing. "Oh, that's ok, I'm used to things not going so well. I'd be disappointed if they didn't." Once again, I was serious and everyone laughed including me. My bloody extract was once again floating in chemicals. She shook and shook and shook and shook. "Uh oh."

She said and shook her head no to the doctor as Nicelee relayed the message to me with a shake of her head. "Try it again." The doctor told the lab tech. I was getting the feeling that what was happening was nearly impossible. On the third try, she declared a minute amount of marrow was floating to the top. But not enough to test properly. "I'm not drilling her a third time," he said. "I'm not putting her through that!" "Use what you have and make it work." He declared. The nurse dressed my two hip holes and gave me instructions on how to mend. I was sore, and for some reason, I felt it down to the bone! Every step hurt as I walked and I declared an "ouch, ouch, ouch," with each step. As I passed all the cancer patients in the waiting room, I nodded and ouched and smiled. Gilda was right; this is the unfunniest thing in the world. But somehow it tends to make you laugh. Some scientist discovered that crying and laughing was an almost identical body reaction; very closely related. I can appreciate that, as I love and hate to do both.

I called the next week for my bone marrow results. I didn't get any further than the lady who answered the phone. "Everything is fine, Mrs. Parenteau." She said. "What does that mean?" I asked her. "The test was negative." She answered. "Negative?" I asked. "Yes, negative." She said with much pride in her voice. "Does that mean I don't have any bone marrow or does that mean I don't have cancer in my bones?" I asked. I really was confused. "Can I speak to Dr. Keith, please?" I asked. "He's with patients now." She answered. "Well, that's ok, because I am a patient too." I guess I was playing a little bit with her. "Would you like to make an appointment to see him?" she asked. "Do I have to pay for an office visit just to come in for test results?" I asked. "If you want an appointment, there is a charge, naturally, for that." She answered. "Oh naturally." I answered. "I guess I'll just accept negative as my answer. Thank you so much for your time." I hung up the phone knowing full well I had not one, but two bone marrow extractions, paid for them and the testing, and due to lack of marrow, they could not be performed. I have more stories such as these, I'm sorry to say. But, if you heard one, you've heard them all! Besides, I'm not supposed to be experiencing any stress anymore.

Psalms 113

Open My Eyes That I May See The Wondrous Things Of Thy Law

March 15, 2002
12:25 pm

Little girl, about 8 years old, walking thru Sears with her 10 year old sister. 8 year old singing, "I love Rock and Roll, because it's good for the soul!……..
God bless little girls everywhere!!!!!!!!!!!!!!!!!!!

unknown
When light is visible and organized into concrete
Objects, reality is material.
When light contains feeling, thought, and intelligence,
Reality is quantum.
When light is completely unmanifest, with no qualities
Anyone can measure, reality is virtual.

Li Po 8th century
You ask why I seclude myself here in my little forest hut?
I just smile and say nothing, listening to the quiet in my soul.
This peacefulness lives in another world
That no one owns.

Change your perspective.

The personality that I feel myself to be dissolved beyond the material level, and with that, I lose the need for the landmarks that I have gathered since birth.

From The Book, God's Most Precious Jewels are Crystallized Tears.

By Barbara Johnson

Lynda and Terri were sisters. Lynda lived in the same town as her mom, and had taken care of her in her continuing illness. Lynda and Terri's mom was coming close to the time of entering the gates of Heaven. Terri had flown home from her out-of-state residence to be with her mom and sister. Lynda and Terri sat by their mother's side as she slowly slipped over the edge into unconsciousness. At the time, Terri lived across country from Lynda and their parents. She didn't spend much time at home, as Lynda did, she wasn't aware of all the little customs and jokes they shared. She also wasn't aware of a favorite song about Heaven, which Lynda and her mom used to love to sing together. "Meet me at the Eastern Gate." As their mother became sicker, and it was apparent she was slipping away, she turned to her daughters and said "I love you." Lynda leaned down to her mother's face and said, "Remember Mom, we'll meet at the Eastern Gate." "What!!" her sister exclaimed. No one told me about meeting at the Eastern Gate!! Who decided it would be the Eastern Gate? If nobody told me, I'd probably be waiting at the Western Gate, asking Jesus, "Where is everybody???" Lynda and her mom began to laugh uncontrollably. Their mother, perhaps hearing her beloved hymn, lay on her bed and laughed her way to Heaven with her daughters laughing at her side.

19

BB GUN

MY BROTHER RECEIVED a bb gun as a gift from our grandfather sometime in the 1950's. It was presented to him at the cottage. I think our dad was more excited than my brother. Cork lifted it from the box and examined his prize. He never asked for one, but he looked at it as a toy, so I think he enjoyed it for the short time it held his attention. He never killed a thing with it; he shot at targets. The very first target was invented in our father's imagination. He ran and grabbed a galvanized pail from under the cottage and ran down the stairs that led to the river. Grandpa had an old wooden rowboat that we paddled around in and fished from. Grandpa had a motor for it, but it was just the kind that hooked over the back of the boat and you started it with a pull cord and steered it with a metal bar that moved back and forth. Grandpa would let us steer but it shook and vibrated so much that as children, we found it hard to control. Dad placed the pail on the last seat of the boat and ran back up the stairs. Grandpa had the gun loaded and Dad snatched it from his father's hands. Raising the gun to his shoulder and aiming, he pulled the trigger. The bb hit the water with a small spit splash. Dad aimed and fired again, spit splash. "The sight is off, Dad." Grandpa laughed as he checked it, then Dad grabbed the gun back. He aimed and fired and hit the side of the boat. Our father handed the gun to my brother who was anxiously waiting his turn. By then I was dancing the jig and waving my arms signaling it was my turn next. Cork took about four shots and hit the boat and the water. "I want a turn!" I couldn't keep quiet and stand still any longer. Immediately my brother began to sputter. "That's my gun, Dad, I don't want her touching it." "Dad, I didn't get anything! I should at least have the chance to hit the pail too." Both of us were right. No one showed me how to hold the gun or position the sight. I only knew what I had picked up from observation. I cocked the gun by putting it between my legs for leverage, raised it to my right shoulder, squinted through the eyepiece and pulled the trigger. KA PING!! I hit the pail. No one was more shocked than me. No, wait a minute; everyone was more shocked than me. I loved shooting. I hit the pail and before anyone could recover from my spectacular display of sportsmanship, I cocked again, raised the gun, found my sight, and pulled the trigger. KA PING!! I did it again!! "Dad, I want my gun back!" Cork screamed. The grown men were not fast in removing it from my arms. I cocked, raised, scoped, and squeezed. KA PING!! Dad and Grandpa were now laughing. Cork walked off just about in tears, and I stood there beaming. "Well, I'll be!" said my grandfather. "How are you doing that?" asked my dad. The expert that I had become, began to simply explain the strategy of my approach. They gave me one more try. The magic spell had been broken. I hit water, spit splash. Cork was inside the cottage eating cookies with Grandma. He gave me a dirty look as I whisked past him and grabbed a cookie from the bag. That was my first and last chance to shoot a gun. I would occasionally go in his room and raise it to my shoulder to find my sight and aim, but I never got to pull a trigger again. I hate guns now; they scare me to death. But I will never forget that feeling of hitting something I was aiming at. I had power for a short while; I had stunned the grown men in my family for a short while. The lesson that I learned that day was: power feels good, control feels good, and being better at something than my brother, also feels good.

I love you Cork!

Love from your sister, Annie Oakley

My Brother, Manley III

By Sharon Parenteau
July 22, 2003

For a sister and a brother, the gap is often wide;
They had to go their own ways, and leave each other's side.
They try to keep in touch, through all the joys and all the tides;
But that seldom happens; as they are both on their own separate rides.
He seems so far away, and her heart breaks when she thinks;
Of the times they shared a bedroom, and a tiny bathroom sink.
She wants to see his face, and touch his full grown hand, but
All she has are memories of times gone by so grand.
He's busy with his family, as she is now with hers, but she yearns to
Turn back time, when his time was always hers.
He was always there beside her, until his college called;
When he left the house forever, the first few days she bawled.
He called with news of "new worlds;" his voice had really changed;
The plans for "Little Sisters" visit were quickly being arranged.
He picked her up in a convertible, his girlfriend at his side;
'Little Sister" rode to Albany in a wind fill backseat,
and took it all in stride.
He sat just in front of her, her eyes glued on his head;
As he took the wheel with command, and flirted with "little Miss Dread"
She used to sit up front with him, always by his side;

She was soon replaced with girlfriends, and then a pretty bride.

It's been a long long time, since they've brushed their teeth together;

She resents the course that life took, and she'll hate it all forever!

Someday they'll rise together; it will seem like one day apart;

They'll share a "new world" together; once again have a brand new start.

But for now he is imbedded and unyielding, deep down in her

"little girl's" heart.

Dear Grandma, Grandpa, and Sharon,

I was just sitting here watching Martin Luther King's funeral and I thought I'd write you a short letter. Vacation is here but it seems as though I've been working harder since I got out. I've been typing since I got up this morning. I'm entering a creative writing contest at school and have been writing all week. The three things in this letter are what I'm entering. The two poems I typed twice, but the story was to long.

Well, how are all of you? We are all fine. Sharon...Scott, our baby brother, was baptized on Sunday and he didn't cry once.

About Easter Sunday, I don't know if we'll be down or not. I have to work Saturday until three and Linda has to work until six. If we are coming down I will call so if you don't hear from us then you know we aren't coming.

I'm getting to be quite a typer, huh Sharon (one-finger style). I thought I'd better send you these poems and this story to show you that you are not the only one in this family who can write. (ha-ha)

If I win they will publish it in the school's literary magazine and I'll send you a copy. Wish me luck. I sure need it!

Well, it's getting late and I have to get ready for work and besides my eyes are starting to hurt and all the keys on the typewriter are running together. So I guess I'll say goodbye for now and write soon.

Love, Cork

THE WALLET
by Manley Tuttle III (Cork)

The man walked into the bar and the beaten storm door slammed behind him. He stood by a torn stool; took fifteen cents from an unjingling pocket, put his hands on the bar and pulled himself onto the stool. He ordered a draft, spun himself in the direction of the nicotine-covered window and peered out.

Across the street stood a row of abandoned gray apartment buildings, trimmed in a washed out red. Many of the windows had been smashed by the neighborhood children. Pigeons rested on the roof; their yellow and white droppings sliding down the side of the wall and covering the broken windows. Slowly he turned back toward his beer, stared at it a moment, then raised his eyes and viewed the bar. He mused at how much the deserted tavern was like himself; musty, broken, and decaying. The smell of stale beer was in every corner. Light was almost non-existent, save for the colors flashing out of a dusty jukebox. He gazed at the bartender with his yellowed tee-shirt and hoary beard. A man at the opposite end of the bar loudly cleared his throat and noiselessly let it fall to the floor.

He turned, unaffected, back to his beer. Then suddenly reached in his back pocket and removed his tattered wallet. He glanced at the empty bill section, smiled a thoughtful smile, then very slowly began removing paper after paper from the dark openings and stacked them neatly on the scratched wood of the bar. He gazed at his past lying in front of him. One by one he picked them up: a shredded license, old business cards, scraps of papers with forgotten phone numbers, and faded pictures. Methodically, he tore them, singly, into tiny squares and let them flutter to the already littered floor. He finished, unnoticed by the others, and sat there. His eyes wandered to the clock over the bar; he looked with blank eyes at it, not even realizing the purpose of the black hands. The walls started spinning and he grabbed and clutched at his untouched beer spilling its contents into a foul, cigarette filled ashtray. The bartender's voice echoed in his ears as if coming from an empty cavern, "Hey, you alright buddy?" He slid from his stool, and the sound of breaking glass crashed into his mind. A warm, wet feeling was enveloping his wrist.

The beaten storm door slammed behind him and his hollow wallet glared up from the bar.

by my brother, Manley Elias Tuttle III

(The two poems are in my first book, I Cry For The Little Girl) by Sharon Parenteau

84

20

PROM GOWN

HERE'S ONE MORE for my brother!

When I was going to the women's clinic a few years back, I was asked, as always, to remove my clothing, except for my socks, put on the paper gown, and then hop up on the table and wait for the doctor. I was alone this day as I waited for my appointment to begin. I felt nervous, as my problems were then multiplying and no one would render it important enough to do testing on me. (Now that I have been diagnosed, all they want to do is tests!) I had put the paper mini gown on with the ties in the back. I tried reaching back to tie it, but couldn't find the paper strips, so I sat there with the "gown" (how do you like what they call them?) continually falling off my shoulders. I always swing my feet like a five year old when I sit on those tables. I do it because I can, I guess. I was nervous. I surveyed the room and spotted paper-drinking cups by the small sink. Maybe a "drink" would calm me down. As only "water" dispensed from the spout, I settled for that. The cup was shaped like a tiny dunce cap. I felt like a dunce in that room wearing a paper mini dress and socks. I filled the cup and raised it to my lips. Just as I did, the side of it caved in and spilled all down the front of my temporary "prom" dress. Now I was not only wearing paper, I was wearing wet, see-thru paper. I filled the cup again, leaned forward over the sink, exposing my bare butt to the hidden cameras I swear they have in there, and took a sip. Still nervous, I needed a new dress and I needed it soon. The doctor would be in at any moment. I searched high and low for a new gown. She had definitely brought this one in with her. (Wouldn't want people stealing them and taking them home for their own personal use.)

I hopped back up on the table and began to swing my legs again. It was hot in there; maybe my paper would dry before anyone came back in. As I sat there, I did something that defies all reasoning. I brushed the front of my gown with my hand, as to remove crumbs from my chest down to my groin. The paper oh so nicely split in half! I tried to pinch it back together. Little pieces ripped between my fingers and they tumbled to the floor. Quickly I removed the gown and put it back on with the ties in the front and the gapping tear in the back. The gown didn't even go all the way around me. Time was wasting. Did I have time to turn it around again, or would I be caught in mid-process, standing there naked as the door opened. I bucked up my nerve and removed the gown. As I shoved one arm in the slit for a hole, the slit separated completely. No armhole! Oh good God this is not happening! I tried to put my arm in the other side and that had also absorbed too much water. I was already nervous, now I was panicked. I jumped up on the table and tried to unfold the wet paper towel gown as big as I could make it. As I got one end of half the gown under my chin and straightened down the front of me, the nurse and doctor walked in. My chin was pinned to my chest; only one breast was covered and I had managed to tuck the other small end between my legs. The looks on their faces were priceless as I began… . "I was getting a drink because my throat was dry and the cup collapsed and spilled and it melted my paper gown here…" "Let me get you another one." Said the nurse as she exited the room. The doctor followed suit. She came back with a neatly folded paper dress that I had grown to despise in those short few minutes. "If you need a drink, get it before you put this on, ok?" She said as she left the room. She was serious! A knock on the door and a "come in" from me began yet another gynecological exam that as women we are blessed to endure.

I had questioned reality long before my dad and my uncle came and took me on a space ride. It is all just too much! God has a wonderful sense of humor and he loves to direct it at me. So Cork, have another laugh on your sister! This is a true story. Even in my wildest imagination, I couldn't have made this one up. I love you!

How do you know God is real?
Look around and see the natural order of creation.
There is tremendous beauty in the simplest things.
Truly look.
If you could see a mountain or a rain cloud for one minute
Without your doubts blocking the way,
The evidence of God would be revealed instantly.
We all see eternity in every direction.
But we choose to cut it into bits and pieces of time and space.
"The all" wants to share. This should give you hope.
Deepak Chopra

"I am that"
"You are that'
"And all this is that"   I AM...................POWER.

I jumped off the ledge of everyday life and landed in a good place where struggle isn't necessary.
I opened the door on the side of eternity.
Galatians 2:20

Eye has not seen, nor ear heard, nor have entered
Into the heart of man, the things which God has

Prepared for those who love him. 1 Corinthians 2:9

Arise; Shine, for your light has come!!!
And the glory of the Lord is risen upon you!
Isaiah 60:1

21

ANTONIO

In my early forties, I had a job working in a jewelry store at our local mall. My health was screaming to me to find out what was wrong and get it fixed. As much as I tried, I was simply dismissed time and time again. Several of these doctor appointments I talked about in my first book, so I will not go through them again.

During this time at "This Fine Diamond Store," also worked a young man from Jamaica. He was a sight to behold. His skin was a perfect rich color. His hair had a slight wave, which he wore combed back off one of the most beautiful faces I have ever seen. He was average build and had teeth and a smile that turned many a girl's head, both young and old. A female customer who met him in the store, a tall redhead, paid him to sleep with her. She came back for more, but he told her no. This young man came with a story.

His mother and father put he and his older brother on a plane to America when he was 16 and his brother was 18. They had an uncle living in New York City and the boys were to stay with him. This only lasted a couple of weeks before they were put out on their own on the streets of NYC. He was very guarded with the information he gave me about the two years before his brother joined the service and he started college. He would say they lived with this person and that person and here and there. He didn't hesitate to tell me he and his brother had been getting financial assistance from the United

States of America ever since their arrival. He simply told the story of two parents who wished more for their two sons, and so they sent them to America. How did Antonio end up in Johnson City, N.Y.? Our government was paying for his education at our local SUNY College. Because of his exceptional looks, he got a job at "This Fine Diamond Store" and was quickly made assistant manager. The manager didn't hesitate to tell the other employees or even our customers that the kid "needed a break". He attended college only part time and worked forty hours a week at the store. He was not a "real" student. He never did homework and barely attended classes. But nonetheless, he was a college student as SUNY funded by our government. So be it. Everyone wanted to dislike him, but it was impossible. With his slight accent and flashy eyes, young and old, male and female were charmed beyond compare.

He liked me. If we were scheduled to work at the same time, he was always by my side. If I had a customer and was selling, he was by my side listening and learning. Next thing I would hear my spiel coming out of his mouth and into his customer's ears. I didn't care. I had age and wisdom on my side, and somewhere deep, deep inside me, God help me, I could hear myself say, "The kid needs a break." He talked my ear off. I answered every question as honestly as I could. I asked him questions. He answered every question as honestly as he felt he could. We talked about our families, our upbringing, childhoods, schools, foods, toys, everything from both cultures from birth to present.

He knew how I felt about what his parents did. "Was Jamaica that bad?' I asked him. "No, no, Jamaica is good! But in Jamaica you must pay for schooling, and you must work hard for money!" he answered. "Antonio, American college students have to pay for their schooling and we have to work hard for our money too!" I said. "No, no, is different, is different. Pay is very low in Jamaica. I send money home every week to my family. Five or ten dollars every week!" he said. "Antonio, do you know how you always watch me sell?" "Yes", he said. "I learned that from my father and from years of being in sales and with years of hit or miss self-teaching. You come here from Jamaica, get a job selling, and they make you assistant manager. You are learning from me, but I have never been an assistant manager in a jewelry store. How do you think that makes me feel? Both my girls paid for their college educations along with our help. You step off the plane and get America handed to you! How do you think that makes me feel?" "I am not the first to do this..." he began. "How well I know that!" I answered. Probably a little too loud. "We all hear how wonderful America is! We all want to come!" He was so enthusiastic and pleased with his success here that I was speechless. What do you say to these people who come here for our great government? "We offer it, but you aren't supposed to actually take advantage of it!" What do you say? Our government starts them in new businesses if they come from a foreign country. Our government finds them jobs even if it means sacrificing one of our local families to be demoted to our welfare program. We must take care of our diversity at all costs. And they mean at "all costs." Aren't there a few women out there who could sit down around a table together and come up with a better plan on managing this huge household called America?

"Antonio, my husband and I won a trip to Jamaica and the locals treated us with great disdain. It was painfully apparent we were not welcome there even as tourists spending large amounts of money in their country. Can you tell me why that is?" "Why would we want strangers roaming all over our towns and beaches! This is our land, give to us to enjoy, not a bunch of filthy strangers littering and using our resources!" "But your country advertises on TV, 'Come to Jamaica and enjoy the splendor'" I answered. "As does yours, Sharon, as does yours. So it's the governments, not the people who wish to share our great lands!"

Antonio and my conversations were always controversial. We argued as much as we shared. We worked together during the OJ Simpson trial when he got acquitted. He let out the biggest YES and roared ALRIGHT! "Tony! You know he did it!" "I know, but his

91

acquittal is payback for slavery." "Slavery, you're not African." "I know, but I'm black."

One day we talked about the species of man. He proclaimed the superiority of the male species. "We are all males, Antonio, we are all males!" He laughed a robust island laugh as he threw his beautiful Jamaican head back, "You are so loco! I thought you were loco, but now it is true!" I let him carry on as long as his ego fed his brain. When he calmed down and was standing face to face with me, waiting for the next ludicrous statement to leave my lips, I imparted a great knowledge upon the young man. "Tony, I am a man! I am a "wo-mbed" man!" A face like his at that moment I have never seen. The wheels of his brain began to spin. His eyes widened as he stared at me. "Wombed." He said over and over again in barely a whisper. "Tony, you are a man, and I am a man with a womb. I have every part as you, and you have every part of me except a womb." We stood together and talked until we matched our different parts into one. From that point on in our relationship, I was his "wo-mbed" Einstein. Few people have figured this out as I have, and I have astounded many with this truth. There is but one small chromosome that separates us and makes us different.

"Sharon, I want to tell you before we all go our separate ways that I have learned a lot from you. You are the best salesman, and I do mean salesman, I have every seen and heard. It has been my pleasure to spend time with you." "Thank you, Toni, same here. Thanks for all the great conversation and thanks for the eye candy." We laughed and hugged as the store we worked at closed and merged with another. I often wonder where America has taken him since his plane ride here so long ago. Is he still here? Did he go back to Jamaica where five dollars is like one hundred? Did we set him up in business somewhere or did he make it "on his own"? God Bless America! God Bless you too, Antonio! And good nite to you Mrs. Kallabash, wherever you are.

22

IN MY HOME

In my home there are many mansions, I go to prepare a place for you. Yet another of Jesus' promises. A few months ago I was taken in my sleep to see my mansion in the "sky". Complete with real estate lady, notebook in arm and smile on face. Nelson and I were led up an impressive set of front steps, steep and long. We arrived in front of two massive solid front doors that opened wide with an easy pull on the handles. We three glided into the foyer and surveyed the house with wonder. From that point on, I was in my new world as I watched sunlight stream in the, floor to ceiling stained-glass windows. They were not the same as church windows; church windows don't even come close to the splendor of what I was seeing. Soft and alive, are the only words I can come up with to describe the colors and the light that flooded into the rooms. (Could this journey have happened hundreds of years ago to someone else and this is where the stained-glass windows originated for churches?) I stood there, my husband at my side, as I became giddy. It was spectacular and it was a mansion! I turned to the real estate lady and gushed, "We can't afford this; this can't be our home!" The lady, standing there in her business suit proclaimed, "You don't have to buy it! It's yours!" She giggled as she found my statement amusing. Looking up into the light, the colors, and the warmth, I began to be pulled backwards at a high rate of speed and found myself back in my bed wide-awake. I mulled over my journey with a smile on my face while Nelson slept soundly beside me. That light, those colors, that warmth, was it all going to be mine in another time and place?

I felt good, whole, and so in love with the Lord. "I love the Lord, I love the Lord!" I could hear my dad shouting in my brain! I love the Lord too, Dad!

23

WEEDS

THE LAST TIME I went to the Oncologist, it was for a blood test. I wanted a red and white count because I was going to try a non-medical non- approved treatment. An acquaintance of ours returned from down south with a machine to cure everything! As I had just read about how the Earth's electromagnetic field produces and stabilizes our beings, it made some sense to me. This person purchased it to treat her Lupus and several other ailments that were annoying her. After I received my blood count, I would be doing something quite high-tech.

My Oncologist was glad to see me. I was one of his favorite cancer patients. My only drawback was my refusal for taking treatments he recommended. But he promised me three years ago that he would see me to the end and continue to doctor me no matter what my choices were..

I had not been in for over a year. He looked in my ears, took my blood pressure, checked my pulse, and knocked my knee. If this would turn out to be a cure for everything, every doctor would be a specialist. He then sat and we began to talk. Mindee, my daughter, accompanied me on this adventure. "How are you? How are you?" he asked in his other side of the world accent. "I hurt here and there, but really, I'm doing really good!" I answered. "Did you ever go see that specialist in Rochester?" he asked. "Holy smoke, you have to be kidding me! Where in the world did you come up with her?" I screeched. He laughed at my antics and said, "What do you mean?" I cut him off right there. "She never looked at my file until I got there! Aaaannnnndddd, she asked me about weeds in my back-yard!" "She asked what?" he said. "She was referring to my cancer as weeds and they needed weed killer then they would come back and I'd need more weed killer..." By then my arms were flailing and I had stood up. He sat across from me laughing. "So she had no good news for you?" he asked. "Only if I wanted to learn horti-culture!" I screeched. "I'm sorry it did not turn out to be anything for you." Dr. Keith said. "That's ok, I never should have gotten my hopes up, that's all." I said. We sat across from each other, me on the examining table, and he in a chair right in front of me. "Sharon, now is the time to get serious, you have put off your treatment for too long now, it is approaching the now or never time." He looked so serious, how long had he practiced in a mirror to get to that face?! "Well, that's why I'm here, I'm going to start a treatment." His face brightened, but I nipped that in the bud real fast. "I'm going to sit with my bare feet on a huge magnetic piece of metal while I hold a glowing plasma tube in each hand, and then I'm going to have electricity enter my body from the energized plasma tubes. This will correct my imbalances caused by being out of tune with the universe, and when that is accomplished, my body would naturally heal itself." At that time it made sense, and I was excited to begin. However, I wanted something to compare the before and after, and all I could come up with was a blood test. I told this all to the good doctor. He laughed at me. I laughed at me too, but I was going to give it a try. He confirmed once again that cancer was nothing to fool with, and I should hesitate no longer. I asked him if there was a pill yet I could take in chemo form. He shook his head no, "There is no magic pill for you; I wish there was." I left feeling unsure that I could believe him, both that there was no pill, and that he wished there was. Did I ever sit with my bare feet resting on the space age wonder cure? Did I hold two glowing plasma tubes as electricity stabilized the chaos in my body? No. I told my acquaintance I was ready, just let me know when she wanted me to come over, she never did. I'd ask her and she'd spout, "Anytime, anytime, just come on over." How could she find my exact frequency if I just popped in at any time? I understood it had to be dialed up. Before the space age machine stage of my life was over, before ever getting to use it, she offered to sell it to me at a reduced price! Was I on candid camera?

I have so many pills, herbs, creams, books, and potions in my kitchen cupboard that I could start up my own cancer cure business. I gave them all the good old American try, but the "other thing" living inside me gets very angry if I try to mess with it. It makes itself unquestionably known. They didn't work and it's not worth the added pain. So we co-exist. When I leave this body, it will no longer survive either. We both must save this sanctuary or we both must sacrifice it.

I choose love

No occasion justifies hatred; no justice warrants bitterness. I choose love. Today I will love God and what and whom God loves.

I choose Joy

I will invite God to be the God of circumstance.

I will refuse the temptation to be cynical... the tool of the lazy thinker. I will refuse to see people as anything less than human beings and my children as children, created by God. I will refuse to see any problem as anything less than an opportunity to see God.

I choose patience.

I will overlook the inconveniences of the world. Instead of cursing the one who takes my place, I'll invite him to do so. Rather than complain that the wait is too long, I will thank God for the moment to pray. Instead of clenching my fist at new assignments, I will face them with joy and courage.

I choose Kindness

I will be kind to the poor, for they are alone. Kind to the rich, for they are afraid. And kind to the unkind for such is how God has treated.

I choose Goodness

I will go without a dollar before I take a dishonest one. I will be overlooked before I will boast. I will confess before I will accuse. I choose goodness.

I chose Gentleness

Nothing is won by force. I choose to be gentle. If I raise my voice may it be only in praise. If I clench my fist, may it be only in prayer. If I make a demand, may it be only of myself.

I chose Self-Control

I am a spiritual being. After this body is dead, my spirit will soar. I refuse to let what will rot, rule the eternal. I choose self-control. I will be drunk only by joy. I will be impassioned only by faith. I will be influenced only by God; I will be taught only by Christ. I Choose self-control.

Love, Joy, Peace, Patience, Kindness, Goodness, Gentleness, and Self-Control.

To these I commit my day.

If I succeed, I will give thanks.

If I fail, I will seek His grace.

And then, when this day is done, I will place my head on

My pillow and rest.

Max Lucado's Book
"When God Whispers Your Name"

24

SING PRAISES

GRANDPA WOULD JOIN us in the last pew on the left, every Sunday morning after he greeted and welcomed the entire congregation. Entering Westover Methodist Church, he stood by the red door and bellowed at everyone. "Welcome, welcome, welcome! And who have we here? What's your name, little lady, little man?" Grandma would shake her head as the three of us sat mostly alone because we had to go so early. "Isn't it a beautiful day!" he said to everyone. He would take the ladies arms and help them up the three steps. Manley Sr. would shake every man's hand. The children were treated the same. The little girls werc hclpcd up the steps; the little boys got a handshake. Grandpa got louder and louder as the church filled up and Grandma's head shook harder and harder. The custodian would climb the bell tower and ring the bell over and over again. If it was Easter, Christmas, or Thanksgiving he had orders to ring it twice as long. Grandpa loved that church bell. Originally it was to tell the farmers in their fields that it was time to worship. Today it is rung for sheer delight. There is something to be said for Sunday morning church bell ringing. It seeks out the very depth of your soul and heart. Maybe in a past life we all were "the farmer" in the field, or the farmer's wife. Something is pulling us back to easier times, safer times, and holier times. We hardly ever hear bells anymore. Our souls are greatly underfed. My granddaughters have yet to ride on a church bell rope. It yanks you off your feet with a jerk and throws you about. You must hang on tight or it will shake you right off. The rope is like a wild horse, when it is finally let loose to do what it was meant to do, it feels freedom!

The day we buried Grandpa... Cork, Scott, Nicelee, Mindee, Nelson and I went up, up, into the belfry of Westover Methodist Church. The ladies put on a church luncheon for our family, as their "greeter" was no more. This was my idea. I had climbed the stairs to the bell many times in my youth and had the rope burns to prove it. About half way up the narrow staircase, the church custodian tried to stop us. I politely told him we were going to each ring our grandfather into heaven. He said no we weren't. The bell could not be rung unless there was a service. I courteously disagreed with him and as we reached the top we were fighting over the rope. I gave him the evil eye my girls know so well and he let go. Scott, my baby brother, had never rang a church bell. Cork and I would "fly" almost every Sunday as our father caught the rope just before we were catapulted over the top of the bell.Scott's feet never left the floor. "Hold the rope up higher, Scott, and it'll pull you right up!" I screeched. His feet still didn't leave the floor. "Let me show you!" I said. As the rope lowered the next time, I grabbed on as high up as I could, expecting to be airborne. My arms were practically jerked out of their sockets! "Here, Mindee, you try! You're little!" I said. I instructed her on the rope flying method. As the rope lowered once again, she grabbed on and pulled, her feet left the floor, a whole three inches! My idea was not working out the way I had planned. I insisted Cork beat the dead horse and pull on the rope. He did, one pull. The custodian smirked at me as we turned to descend the bell tower. We had failed; we had failed to be children anymore. No matter how hard we tried, we were not children any more.

When Cork and I first came to live with Grandma and Grandpa, the seating on Sunday morning was Cork, Grandma, Me, then Grandpa. The service always started with a song. There were two hymnals in the book holder in front of us. Cork and Grandma shared and Grandpa and I shared. When the organist began to play the hymn, I could tell it was going to be a good one. It started so dramatically. The last long chord held and… it was time to sing. Grandpa sang so loud and off tune that I just stared up at him. That was my first mistake. He always added extra notes and divided the one-syllable words into three or four parts. He gave each song its own little flare. Listening was hard enough, but to watch his mouth was a killer! I began to laugh and I couldn't stop. He gave me the evil eye. I only found it funnier. He shoved the hymnal closer to my face. "Sing!" he whispered. I wasn't singing, I was laughing and that made me laugh even harder. I couldn't escape because he was on the end. I looked at Cork and Grandma. Would they let me out of there? No, by the looks on their faces! Grandpa just kept on singing loud, off tune, and adding his extra special touches. I tried pinching my forearm. Ouch! It hurt, but that was funny too. I dreaded the next song, and then the last song. As I grew and got older, my spot was always next to my grandfather in church. As a young teen, I just mouthed the words. God forbid if one of my friends were to look back and see me singing church songs. I refused to close my eyes during prayer. I preferred to study faces then. As I grew older, my grandfather's singing grew from funny to embarrassing. However, when I knew my church going days were coming to an end because I was engaged and getting married, I began to mimic my grandfather's singing in church. He looked at me with question marks for eyes. I held my head high and belted out "Amazing Grace." As we stood there together, singing the way he had always wanted me to, he was pleased. My future was hidden from me. Had I mocked him on purpose because I was soon to be free from attending church? Was he pleased I was singing because he knew what was in my future? Now I am in the middle of the middle of my life. Somewhere deep down inside of me I "know" what is in store for the whole human race. Does the knowledge come with age? Did it come with age for my grandfather, too? Did he know the nineteen year old singing next to him that day, would confront many trials and tribulations? I can still hear him sing how the Lord saved a wretch like him and it still makes me laugh. But now I laugh through my tears. I miss my Grandpa!

ANGRY

(Schoolwork from 11th grade, I got an 85 on this. It was written before I remembered the abductions.) (For more information, read my first book)

I lay here, not moving. The very thought of this happening to me makes me shutter. Is this true? Could this really be happening to me? The silence of the night falls upon my room with horror, and the darkness around me shortens my breath.

I lay here, thinking…thinking so hard that my head fills with pain and I feel like screaming………loud…oh so loud as to waken the whole world and tell them of this happening. I lay here…I hear things………strange things…things I've never heard before. But this night…ah yes…this night I hear them……….and, oh so loud to my ears……..and so strange. Can't they hear them?……Can't you hear them?…….. Why can't they hear them, too…? I lay here…oh so still…….listening……constantly listening for them to come…….they are coming……yes……they are coming…….they will be here soon……I can hear them……..I lay here……..waiting……..the sweat pours from my skin, and I feel cold. Colder than I have even been before. I move……oh so slight…….as to remove some of my covering. They feel so heavy……..I can't move they feel so heavy!……the noises go on…….I can hear them coming…….closer and closer and closer…….it will not be long……ah yes, I hear the door now……..It wasn't locked?…….I wonder how

102

many came…this time...their footsteps up the stairs sound many…….. (Step #)..6..7…8…9…

Sharon Tuttle Parenteau

25

THE LORD IS MY SHEPHERD

I̲F̲ ̲Y̲O̲U̲ ̲C̲A̲N̲'̲T̲ sleep, this is the perfect answer. There is something out there in the hemisphere that hears the 23rd Psalm and comes and sprinkles pixy dust in your eyes. It has never failed for me. During the days following my accurate diagnosis of Cutaneous T-Cell Lymphoma, I was desperate for some kind of brain relief. From my childhood in Sunday school, came forefront in my mind, the 23rd Psalm.

I began to repeat it over and over again, desperately trying to find "the answer" that would take away my misery. I said it so fast and so desperately that I became more agitated and desperate than before I started. This was not my answer. I said the Lords Prayer, and the ending benediction to each Sunday service that my father said for years. No, I wasn't feeling better yet. My mind kept going back to the 23rd Psalm. I didn't want to get caught up in that merry-go-round again! My brain had its own idea. It started in again, only this time my brain slowed down enough so I could ponder the meaning.

The Lord is my Shepherd, I shall not want.

(The Lord watches over me. What more could I ask for?)

He maketh me to lie down in green pastures:

He leadeth me beside the still waters.

(Picture yourself to calm yourself sitting in the tall grass and wading in still waters.)

He restoreth my soul!

(He has the ability to transform the troubled mind and soul of the most destitute. When you say, He restoreth my soul; feel your inner self lighten and be thankful.)

He leadeth me in the path of righteousness for his namesake.

(God wants us to do good, to do right, and he will lead us if we will only let him. Give it all over to God. The better we do, the better he feels.)

Yea, though I walk through the valley of the shadow of death,

(on Earth we are always shadowed by death. It is all around us and we can't escape it.)

I will fear no evil, for thou art with me.

(God will calm your fear and your spirit as you live in such uncertainty. Give it over to Him to take care of.)

Thy rod and thy staff they comfort me.

(As Jesus protected the sheep in his field, he also protects us. God has supplied us with our own weapons to fight anything that might come along. We have His promise and His constant love in our heart.)

Thou preparest a table before me in the presence of mine enemies.

(God shows us His love and boldly dismisses evil when we go on with life as it is presented to us. Remember, as a Lamb of God, our tall grass and cool water is located among the lions.)

Thou anointh my head with oil, my cup runneth over.

(You give me all and more than I need to get through this time joyously. You never leave my side. If I glance over my left shoulder at any given time, I can see you hovering there, and I thank you for that.)

Surely goodness and mercy shall follow me all the days of my life and I will dwell in the house of the Lord forever.

(God has not taken care of me and watched over me, to just let me go at the end. He wants me home. He wants everyone home to complete his wholeness again.)
AMEN

Benediction
The Lord bless and keep you.
The Lord make His face to shine upon you and be gracious unto you.
The Lord lift up his countenance upon you....... and give you peace.
AMEN

The Lord is my light and my salvation! Of what
Shall I fear! The Lord is the strength of my
Life! Of what shall I be afraid?
Psalm 27:1

Be anxious for nothing.
But by prayer and with thanksgiving,
Let your requests be made known to God.
And the peace of God, which surpasses all under
standing, will guard your hearts and minds
Through Jesus! Philippians 4:6-7
Call to me, and I will answer you. I will
show you great and mighty things, which
you do not know. Jeremiah 33:3

26

DO YOU TAKE...............

During our stay in Rome, PA; once a year the two Protestant churches got together for a combined day of worship. The Presbyterian Church was kitty corner from our Methodist parsonage. It was big and brick and had beautiful windows and a tall steeple. My father's Methodist Church was on the outskirts of town; made of clapboard, painted white, (a long time ago) and had small, stained-glass windows and a short steeple with a bell tower on top. You've seen a million of them as you travel the backroads of America. My father was not happy about the combination day, but it had been done long before we came to that church and I'm sure it continued long after we left. Dad was not afraid to talk openly at home about anything. It was ok to talk in front of my brother, but not in front of me. I am a consument storyteller. I love to watch people's eyes as I spin my tale! "Betty, this fries my butt! This is the last thing I want to do! Those people have it all wrong! How can I, in all good conscience, participate in this farce!" he ranted. "You haven't any choice. It's just one day, you can get through it." She said. He said a lot more things about that religion and its followers, and I heard it all!

Sunday morning "unity" was upon us. We all dressed in our Easter Sunday best and trooped across the street to the bigger, nicer, prettier church. Reverend Truman sat up front behind the alter along with the Reverend of their church. Two "more fake" smiles could

107

not be found for miles around! Up and down. Up and down. Both men took turns reading passages from the Bible, announcing the next song, and conducting prayers. My father's head tipped up to the heavens; he prayed like never before. Eyelids fluttering as each praise this, and praise that, was released from his mouth coming straight from his heart. Would some of the "fancy church" goers end up at our church next Sunday?

Mom and Cork and I sat in the front row pew opposite the "other minister's wife and kids." We all glanced back and forth at each other as our fathers changed positions of superiority at the pulpit. Before the end of the service, I felt like we were competing with each other. But I never figured out what the reward or prize was supposed to be. We entered the church inferior, just because our church was too small for both congregations.

All was fine until the very end. I was handling the new experience well (even though all the stuff my dad said about the "other" religion was soooo off base!) The other Reverend, the one who had it all wrong, stepped up to the front of the church bypassing the podium, to boot. Soft music rang from the organ. The "other" Reverend raised his arms and closed his eyes. Hey, he stole that from my dad!! Maybe my dad was right, these were not normal people! As he raised his arms and closed his eyes, a new combination of words came out of his mouth that I had never heard before. "If you take Jesus Christ as your Lord and Savior, if you believe the only way to Heaven is through Christ's shed blood, if you feel it deep down in your heart that you are a sinner and not worthy of the washing in the blood, than come, come now to Jesus Christ..... don't be afraid, come forward now and receive Christ into your heart and wash your sins away! He was hollering all of this by then! I was scared to death! My father never raised his voice in church unless he was rejoicing. Now I needed to come forth to be washed in the blood of Christ to get rid of sins? I knew even at the young age of six, that Christ's body didn't hold enough blood to wash away all my naughtiness!

People began to stroll up to the front of the church, some heads bowed, some held high, but all hands were clasped in front of each one of them. I really noticed that. Their hands rested at the ends of their arms with their entwined fingers together.

I began to glance back and forth at the two families sitting opposite each other in the front pews. They were moving! I looked at my mom and brother. They sat still, back straight, heads up, and there again, hands crossed and folded in their laps. I scooted my butt to the back of pew and held it there with all the butt muscle I could muster. I looked straight ahead and folded my hands in my lap. I was not going anywhere either! As I sat there feeling so out of place, I sought out my father's mostly hidden face as he sat in a chair behind the pulpit. He had scooted his chair over further.... I was sure of it! He was literally hiding. He looked at me with sad apologizing eyes. I knew instantly that I was going to be ok. It seemed to take forever for all who came to Christ that morning to get there. The saddest music was whining from the majestic organ. Like a bolt of lightening coming from God knows where, a new revelation came to me. I had been under the impression that Jesus had been handed to me on a silver platter! Compliments of my father, Rev. Tuttle! I never dreamed I had to actually do something to deserve his love. Sometimes, even today, I feel he came to me so easily. I never felt like I had to approach him. I swear I feel him over my left shoulder all the time. I've been praying since birth. If you count folding your hands, bowing your head and closing your eyes, praying. That's as far as I went as a child. I considered it a grown up obligation to pray. I just went along for the ride. Today when I pray to Jesus, I feel him come to me. I don't feel myself reaching to touch him. Maybe my dad was right. Maybe testimony and being washed in the blood isn't necessary to be saved. I've never approached the front of a church during any kind of demonstration of faith. However, I have dropped to my knees several times in my mind, in awe and gratitude.

It was a bright sunny day when the entire congregation exited the church. Every one of us walked through the same door. Some had been "washed" and some of us had not. As I looked around the smiling, mulling people out front talking to each other (as if nothing significant had just happened to some of them,) I was struck by the fact that I couldn't tell the Presbyterians from the Methodists. I sauntered over to my mother as she stood speaking to a young woman from the "other half." My mother looked down at me, looked up, and took an instant replay. "Sharon Evonne, what have you been doing to your hair?" she asked. Mentally, I had been pulling it out by the roots during the finale, but I didn't know that would show on the outside. Mom began to lick her fingers and work each pin curl back into place. She licked and smoothed so fast, that it appeared that she was eating my hair! "Sharon Evonne, what am I going to do with your hair?" she screeched. The pretty young woman suggested that she might try parting it on the other side of my head. Just then my father walked up to join us. "You know, that might not be a bad idea." She said to the woman as she looked at my head. As my father was approaching, I glanced up at the lady and noticed her part was on the opposite side of mine. "Mommy, you can't part my hair on THAT side." I said. "Well, why not?" she asked. I had to word this just right so as to get my point across. "Because that's the way the Presbyterians part their hair!" everyone in earshot began to laugh. My dad began to double over in hysteria. All week he had been "talking down" the church across the street, and now they wanted me to become a Presbyterian! That story has been repeated and repeated so many times that I am sure it is still reverberating off the black hole in outer space. "Oh Sharon, you're such a character!" was repeated to me by young and old. When I was a character..... I was just like my dad. Most of the time, what I said just came out. Something like divine cleverness, I guess. The question wasn't then and isn't now, "Do I take Jesus Christ as my Lord and Savior?" the question is, "Does he want me?"

110

Commune with your own heart on your bed, and be still.
Be still and know that I am God.
Said by God

As a Marathon Runner enters the "zone"
So can I...
The runner no longer feels pain as part of his experience.
The God of peace is detached.
The runner's mind stops fighting and struggling. The God
of peace is calm.
The zone makes one feel immune to harm. The God of peace
offer consolation.
Winning and losing are no longer a driving force. The God
of peace is conciliatory.
The runner's mind quiets down. The God of peace is silent.
In the zone one expands beyond the limits of the body, touch-
ing the wholeness and oneness of everything. The God of
peace is meditative.
The God of peace isn't found by diving within so much as
he rises.
Deepak Chopra   "When the Time is Right"

I used to be inside the movie, but now I am sitting in the
audience watching it.

Psalm 4: Now I shall lie down in peace, and sleep, for you
alone, O Lord, makest me unafraid.

If you find your own inner quiet, the issue of violence is
solved, at least for you personally.

111

Stare at the blue of the sky and then look beyond it. The whole intent is to go past the senses in order to find the source.

27

RED LIPSTICK

Nelson, I and the girls never called Grandma Douglas before we went to visit her. When we arrived, she would always be doing something; never sitting down. We'd find her outback patting her flowers lovingly and pulling weeds, or she would be in the kitchen making yet another one of her exceptionally original, exotic dessert creations. Two days ago I myself took a chocolate cake mix, a brownie mix, and a frozen package of raspberries and baked a cake. I put the required eggs and oil in and added water until it reached the consistency of cake batter. It took longer to bake than a cake; I thought it would never get done. After I looked at it, I decided to call it some kind of torte. I iced it with butter cream frosting and solidly covered it in fresh coconut. Everyone thought it was delicious. Lately I am bored with the usual, the predictable, and when an adventure turns progressive, I am not surprised. Grandma had creativity, but few channels to explore it. I am a lot like my mothers, mother was.

Grandma was always glad to see us. We would talk a little while by the flowers and then she would invite us in for a cold drink. Grandma would then disappear for about five minutes. We four would sit on the couches and survey the room. Grandchildren's pictures were all over the walls. Knick-knacks sat here and there, given to her a billion years ago. There were enough throw pillows to choke a whale. In the corner sat her prized, small, fake wood, electric organ. Soon Grandma would emerge from the back end of her mobile home in full-face makeup. We were not supposed to notice anything different about her, but boy; you couldn't help it.

Grandma Douglas was born with no top lip to speak of. It must have been a real defect in her eyes. As the years multiplied, her top lip fell inward as she aged. The skin above her top lip, beneath her nose, seemed to be caving into itself. The "now" peaks and valleys of her lips were carefully constructed from a tube of bright red lipstick. Grandma gave new meaning to voluptuous lips. Her peaks reached and entered each nostril. The corners of her lips were rimmed with red like the top of a margarita glass is with salt. Two perfect, bright pink rouge moons encircled her bare cheekbones. The skin had long since surrendered to gravity. Her eyebrows were arched like the cover girls on the 1932 war posters. We and our girls sat there trying not to look and not to laugh, if we did look. She had come into herself in that short five minutes in front of her bathroom mirror. Chattering, she made her entrance into the living room carrying a tray of drinks. Her "special drink" was all her own creation. (back then) She mixed iced tea and fruit juice together in a tall glass of ice. Grandma Douglas was indeed the first "Snapple lady". Her daughters and granddaughters laugh and sigh as we think of what "could have been". Grandma, Grandma, Grandma, who were you? Why didn't someone take your iced tea and run with it? Because it was not to be........all things come to those who wait.......are people still saying that? When was the last time any of us waited for anything except a paycheck? What went wrong? When were we supposed to stop evolving? During the Renaissance time? During the time of cowboys and Indians? Right before the Iron Age? Surely before computers. Computers.... we figured out how to duplicate the brain..........I believe in evolution, but evolution with common sense. I think we were created and continue to be altered. Our two-year-old granddaughter could operate a computer mouse the first time she touched one. I was all over the screen for a few days. Our children are born angry. It is twice as hard to give them a happy life. We are not protecting them from evil anymore and we are clicking a remote and even inviting it in. No one has any time anymore. Children are left to fend for themselves. We are self-destructing......... either by choice or by demand. I don't know which is true......... Reality has taken on a whole new meaning for civilization. It cannot be the true reality. If it were, God would be the center, and He is not. All any of us can do now is "hold on," it's going to be a bumpy ride.

Laugh and the world laughs with you. Cry.................. and you have to blow your nose.   A first grade child

The Four Stages of Life
1. You believe in Santa Claus.
2. You don't believe in Santa Claus.
3. You are Santa Claus.
4. You look like Santa Claus.
By???

Jesus wanted His disciples to be "in the world but not of it." Detached in the sense that they remained motivated to lead a worthy life. This leaves only nowhere. And that is where we should be. There is a tremendous secret to this nothing and nowhere.
"The Cloud of Unknowing" written anonymously in the 14th century.

Thus the hunt is on!! And if you keep to your plan, rejecting outward answers over and over, never giving up on your belief that the hidden goal is real, eventually your seeking bears fruit!!! Your inside work is silent. Thus the balancing act Jesus referred to as being in the world but not of it!!

The soldiers sacrificing his life on the front lines can't afford to blame.....what's the point? The enemy is just him in another man's body....

If you love these following lines from the great Persian Rumi, you definitely understand how the inner world can be more thrilling than anything outside.

To be a hunter of the knowledge of God.....
The chase is all the more challenging when the prey leaves no tracks in the snow.......

There are no victims.
Everything is well ordered, things happen as they should.
Random events are guided by higher wisdom.
Chaos is an illusion; there is total order to all events.
Nothing happens without a reason.

Monday, March 4, 2002   3:10 pm

Reading a book at my desk, at my job, at the mall.
Elderly man walking by..... "Is that a good book?"
I held the book up so he could see the title.
"How to Know God", by Deepak Chopra.
Elderly man..... "Must be lots of wisdom in that book!!"
I said, "I'm trying."
He said, "If you have to make friends, might as well make good ones!!"

28

THE MINUET

I CLEARLY REMEMBER THE first time I saw and learned about the Minuet. It was a television show about that period in time. The jist of it is that "back then" people would get up in the morning, dress in their finest wear, eat breakfast, and then gather in the ballroom to dance the minuet; and it was still morning! Still, to this day, it boggles my mind and yet somewhere deep down inside of me, I remember doing just that. What must life have been like then. Men and women alike; dressed, ate, and danced all morning to music. If we think of what we know to be at the beginning of all creation: with dinosaurs, cave men; then warriors, pirates, cowboys, gladiators, biblical times, and all times of strife; at any given moment you could have been eaten, clobbered, harpooned, stabbed, shot, beheaded, or fed to the lions. Consider after all that existence that was reality, to evolve into what was next to come................

Then came the powdered wigs, ruffles, bosoms, bustles, and the Minuet. Who were these people? Where did they come from? Surely they were not evolved from our species. Why did we stop minueting? How come no one has started a Minuet Breakfast Club? I close my eyes and I am there, dressed to the nines and gently being guided by a gentleman around the outer perimeter of the ballroom. We smile and nod to each other as I raise my fan to cover half of my face as I blush. My breasts are spilling out of the top of my dress,

117

yet I play the shy, innocent, weaker sex. Soon I must sit, as a case of the vapors overtakes me. A crowd gathers around and doesn't leave until I assure all, that I am nicely recovering. My gentleman stays and holds my hand until we can resume the dance. In the movies they never show us what these people did in the afternoon. Probably tea and then a nap. I think Heaven will have a building reserved for those who wish to do the Minuet every morning. I won't be one of them. I will be with the children or on the beach with an umbrella drink.

I wanted to name Mindette, Minuette, just because of what it represents. I was afraid everyone would call her Minnie. I wish now I had followed my first instinct and named her Minuette, if just for the sheer mystery and pleasure of it!

So French, you know!

Christmas
By J.B. Phillips

A senior angel is showing a very young angel around the splendors of the universe. They view whirling galaxies and blazing suns, and then flit across the infinite distances of space until at last they enter our particular galaxy of 500 billion stars. As the two of them drew near to the star we call our sun and to its circling planets, the senior angel pointed to a small rather insignificant sphere turning very slowly on its axis. It looked as dull as a dirty tennis ball to the little angel, whose mind was filled with the size and glory of what he had seen. "I want you to watch that particular one," said the senior angel, pointing with his finger. "Well, it looks very small and rather dirty to me," said the little angel. "What's special about that one?" To the little angel, Earth did not seem too impressive. "Well," said the senior angel, "That small planet is the renowned "visited planet." "Do you mean that our great and glorious Prince…went down in person to that fifth-rate little ball?" "Why should he do a thing like that?" "Do you mean to tell me that He stooped so low as to become one of those creatures of that floating ball?" "I do, for as strange as it may seem to us, He loves them. He went down to visit them and to lift them up to become like Him." "God," said the senior angel, "took on the shocking confines of a baby's skin, the ominous restraints of mortality. He is the image of the invisible God, the first born over all creation. He is before all things, and in Him all things hold together."

Could it be true, this Bethlehem story of a creator descending to be born on one small planet? If so, it is a story like no other. Never again need we wonder whether what happens on this dirty little tennis ball of a planet matters to the rest of the universe. Little wonder a choir of angels broke out in spontaneous song, disturbing not only a few shepherds, but the entire universe……….

29

DOG TAGS

Every morning that I go to work, I rifle through my jewelry drawer for the six small pieces of gold I wear. I tried to sell all of it after I was diagnosed. I had tremendous medical bills to pay. Later, my husband cashed in his retirement fund to get us out of medical debt. He accompanied me to several used gold and jewelry pawn-shops. He had purchased most of the items for me, that I was trying to sell. He was embarrassed; I was angry. I knew I wasn't going to get anywhere near the value of the pieces to even make a dent in my bills. At the time, I was going through my meager existence phase. The first dealer told me he would give me $800.00 for my appraised, $6,000.00 twenty-fifth wedding anniversary ring. He said my two gold bracelets were worth under $100 each. My grandmother's black onyx ring was not even in the running. I told him how old it was, but he wasn't impressed. We got the same answers at all four places we went. I was even going to sell my grandmother's ring I had been wearing since I was a young teenager. What used to fall off my ring finger now only fits my pinky. I went home with all my jewels intact and now I am glad with the way things worked out. I'm materialistic once again. I will pass down my belongings to my daughters and granddaughters.

My jewelry drawer is also full of junk. Broken chains, sterling silver, and gifts I don't wear but can't part with. It seems that every morning my grandmother's ring is almost impossible to find. Did I lose it yesterday and not realize it? So far, it is found and placed back on my right pinky finger.

This morning, as I was once again digging, my hand rested upon a silver, oval, flat piece of metal with writing on it. It was issued by the Masonic Temple. The ID number was 609. The name on it was Manley Elias Tuttle Sr., 103 Endwell Street, Johnson City, NY. It must have been in the box my grandfather gave me the same day he gave me the family photo albums before he died. I decided to take the time that morning to get my glasses and take it over to the window and read what it said. This is when I saw my grandfather's name and address and the Masonic symbol. I turned it over in my hand and there, right down the center of the dog tag, was my maiden name. My little girl name. It was then that I remembered wearing it around my neck on a pull chain type necklace. I always tried to count the tiny balls, but I didn't know how to count that high at the time.

World War II had ended and then came the Korean conflict. Nuclear war was the latest threat. We could be annihilated at any moment. In kindergarten, we were taught to crawl under our desk and cover our heads with our arms. Was it ignorance or kindness, I'll never know.

My grandfather was a Mason. A member of a secret society associated with religion. As a little girl, I heard of riding goats as an initiation. This was not true. Masons make no bones about being privileged to knowledge that cannot be shared. The women's order is called Eastern Star. I am absolutely convinced that this society has something to do with something that comes from the sky, something unearthly. I wish I could become a Mason and find out.

My dog tag was worn throughout the nuclear war threat time of the 1950's. People were building bomb shelters in their backyards. People were paying people to build bomb shelters in their backyards. Now we know no amount of steel and no amount of food would have preserved us from the bomb. There were always rumors of this family or that family that had a secret bomb shelter built in their backyard. Children came to elementary school bragging of ownership of one. Do I hate them or do I befriend them? Such a dilemma for little children.

My grandfather apparently wanted me returned to him in case of war. We lived in Pennsylvania and he in New York, but there was his name and address on the other side of mine. Was he expecting to receive a whole little girl or a war-torn little body. What was in his head in 1955? Had I known from the beginning that I would be his little girl until the day he died? Had he known we were connected by some unseen force that neither of us could break? Had he known I would grow to love him like a father? Had he known my heart would never be the same after he was gone? I think we both knew, everyone around us knew. The little boy playing stickball had me buried in his heart just waiting for my time to appear. The homely, funny, little girl with pink shoes on (compliments of my EJ grandfather) when not one other girl in my town had any. I still have the dog tag 48 years later. Our names are forever etched upon it. Nothing left to chance. "Does your father know you are buying that?" There was always a nickel on his dresser. Oh how I have been taken care of!

30

MY GREAT UNCLE GEORGE

After Grandma Tuttle died, Grandpa and I finally became relaxed with each other. He no longer looked at me with resentment or anger. He looked at me as an adult. That's when we really got to know each other. I remember at one of our lunches with him, Aunt Jan, and I, he asked me if I wanted a drink. Not just a drink: but a D R I N K. He and Jan would always have one martini with extra olives. Grandpa would smack his lips really loud in the restaurant and embarrass Jan and I, but we were just so glad to have him enjoying himself. He had become our spoiled little boy; he got everything he wanted and he was being mothcred by two of his favorite females on earth! I never could bring myself to have a drink in front of him. In the back of my mind, I guess I thought it must be a trick or some kind of a test that I still must pass. We were finally enjoying each other's company. He told me several stories about his childhood and his parents and the farm he lived on; I consumed his every word. One afternoon, I brought up the subject of Grandma's sister, Annamae's husband, Uncle George. "That's really something about Uncle Georges' childhood, isn't it?" I said. "What about it?" Grandpa asked. "You know, the way he was left on someone's front steps in a laundry basket, and how those people just took him in and raised him." I answered. "Who in tar nation told you that?" he looked at me and said. "He did!" I said. "And you believed him?"

"It's the truth, why wouldn't I believe him?" Grandpa laughed and just stared at me. "He wasn't left on someone's front porch in a basket!" "Well, he told me he was!" "He was an orphan, but he wasn't left on anyone's front porch." I was so disappointed. Maybe because I wanted to believe someone would actually be so kind, or because it was such a great story to share. Uncle George got up every morning, went to work, and handed his paycheck to his wife at the end of every week. She had been signing his name to it so long that the family joke was, "We hope Mom doesn't die before Dad does, because he could never get his paycheck cashed ever again. Uncle George is Barbara and Esther's father. They have researched the family tree of his heredity and discovered more of his beginning, but all that doesn't matter to me. He was the funny man in our family. When any child entered his home, he'd bellow; "What are you doing here, you three-eyed, two-nosed, bow-legged, knock-kneed, pigeon-toed, cross-eyed, hunched-over, pot-bellied, short-fingered, ect., etc., whipper snapper was always the last two words. He would always go on for a good one or two minutes. Every time, it was all new material. He surely could have been a stand-up comic today with his quick wit. We would all laugh as he went on and on and on. When he was done, he'd approach the child and pretend to do a one-two punch to the gut as we squirmed backwards and bent forward. He was a great man!

Aunt Mae and Uncle George would rent the cottage down from ours, and we would all gather at one or the other. It just so happened that during the spring thaw this particular year, a big tree became lodged in the middle of the river in front of their rented cottage. Uncle George told Esther and I that there would be fish gathered all around that tree stump. He loaded us in the boat after Esther and I grabbed poles off the cottage porch. Uncle George had already overturned one big shovel full of dirt from under a shade tree and the worms began to squirm. He grabbed at them as they immediately began to burrow down. We had our worms in a can and Uncle George and his two darlings were off to catch some fish. We tied the boat to the exposed part of the tree sticking out of the river and had our first baiting a hook lesson. We wanted to fish so badly that Esther and I came up with a perfect baiting solution. We each grabbed a tissue from our shorts front pocket and began to fish in the worm can. Uncle George put the kybosh on that in one short second. "Oh no, if you want to catch fish, you have to pay the price. Grab a worm and hold it between your thumb and first finger. Esther and I squealed and scrunched up our noses and fished through the dirt in the can. Uncle George was having none of that, either. "Cut the noise and cut the faces." He showed us how to hook the worm through the back of its neck and then once again into the middle of its body. "This way the worm can squirm and the fish will think it's on vacation." Esther and I just looked at each other." We hooked as the "brown stuff" oozed out of the worm. Yes, he sure was still able to squirm. All three of us cast our lines in at the same time. One on each side of the boat, and one off the back. We all got strikes almost simultaneously. They were sunfish. And they were beauties too. He showed us how to remove the hook from the fish's mouth. Most of the time, we didn't even have to re-bait the hook; the worm was still on it and still squirming. We filled a pail in no time.

The next lesson was to learn how to clean them. We rowed back to shore and Uncle George got a stack of newspapers. We all sat in the front yard under a shade tree and he began the task. Reaching into the pail and retrieving the first fish, he slit it from neck to tail and pulled it open and began to scrape out the insides. Esther asked her dad if it was ok if we went to the bathroom. When we were out of earshot, she told me it was a plan to get out of the cleaning lesson. We were off playing something else and the fish were forgotten for now. The fish were forgotten...until we woke the next morning. Aunt Mae was sautéing the white flesh in drawn butter that had been lightly dusted with flour, salt and pepper. It was the best breakfast I had ever tasted! We ate and she kept it coming until all four of us had plenty to satisfy our morning appetite. The first thing she and I wanted to do was go fishing again. "Daddy, can we go fishing again?" Esther asked her dad. "I don't care. You can go by yourselves, you both know what you need to do, don't you?" We both shook our heads enthusiastically. We got the shovel and turned the earth. We grabbed at the bait and we put it in a can. We grabbed the fish pail and ran to the boat. She and I each took one oar and maneuvered out to the stump. We dropped anchor and grabbed our poles. We got a worm and haphazardly stuck the hook through it once just anyplace it happened to land. We had hit after hit. Every person in every cottage in the area knew there were two little girls out there fishing. We squealed and squawked and delighted in each new catch. We filled the pail in no time. We were even so bold as to depart the boat and sit on the tree stump in the middle of the river. We were in paradise and it was located in Windsor, NY in the middle of the Susquehanna River. We went back to shore and showed the pail to her dad, my Great Uncle. "Get the newspaper and get going on the cleaning, then take them in to your mother to refrigerate. Do you need me to get you both started?" We both chimed. "No, we can do it." He walked away as we both stared into the bucket of sunfish. "Let's let them live a little longer?" I said. Esther couldn't have agreed with me more. We placed the pail "behind" the big oak tree and were off for a swim. Afternoon turned to evening and evening to bedtime and then morning. It was a morning we were soon not to forget. We did not wake to the smell of butter drenched white flaky fish, frying in the pan. We approached the kitchen and there sat her dad. We wanted to run, but we were sure he could have caught us easily, one in each hand. "Mom, we forgot about the fish." Said Esther. Her mom glanced at her husband and kind of gave us a grim look. I was wondering if I might be able to run down along the riverbank to my cottage and to safety. I decided to stay and take the medicine. Our fishing lesson a couple of days ago also included lessons on ethics, the value of life, survival of the fittest, and the circle of life. We had broken every law as surely as Moses was sitting at that breakfast table. "Where's the fish you caught yesterday?" Uncle George asked. "Under the shade tree." We both pretty much

126

said at the same time. "Shall we have a look at em?" he asked us. With heads bowed, we walked to the "hanging tree." All three of us just stood, heads bowed, watching for a speck of life in a bucket full of belly-up fish. We would still be standing there if Esther's father had not broken the ice. "Well, what have we here?" Esther and I stood with our little chins glued to our chest. "Girls, we only kill what we eat." Did we kill something!! We didn't even dare glance sideways at each other. "Well?" he asked us. "Well?" (is that a question, I wondered?) life was void from the pail; not even a twitch of a tail. How long was he going to make us stare at this bucket that had begun to stink? "You broke one of God's laws." He said. I knew it, I knew it, it did have something to do with Moses. "Was fishing fun?" he asked us. We both managed to shake our heads yes with chins still glued to chest. "The two of you have to carry that pail of dead fish down to the river and dump it, and don't do it right out front either, and don't dump it too close to shore. And girls, no more fishing for you." Esther picked up the pail and we never looked back...or up. Now we had to figure out how far down the river we had to go, and how much we had to wade out to empty the dead fish. It wasn't so much fun anymore. We were ashamed and mortified that we had killed but not consumed. Esther and I never fished together again. I have never fished at all since those two fun days. The next spring the downed tree was no longer lodged in the middle of the river. Catching a fish would never ever be that easy again so we never even tried. Is that why we disregarded our lessons? Had God and nature made it too easy for two little girls that lazy summer week? Was He watching our glee with each new cast? The circle of life is as I consume, I too shall be consumed. She and I now, are two sunfish swimming in the biggest fish bowl imaginable. Our water, air, food, and environment is slowly killing us too. Cancer has made itself welcome to each of us. The fish in the bucket didn't have a chance to get back to their home in the river. Two little girls held their fate. God holds our fate in his hands. I never forgot those two days with my Uncle George and the wisdom he shared with us that I have applied to so many more things in my life than fishing. Could there really be just one law, one rule that must not be broken. Could it be that easy? God assures us that it is. Our journey here is to discover what that one magnificently simple rule is and then go live it.

After Uncle George retired, he would follow the railroad tracks from his home in Westover to Johnson City every afternoon. They could have had the newspaper delivered, but he liked this time alone. He grew up near the railroad, and enjoyed the extreme shortcut to buy a newspaper. On this particular day, for reasons God only knows, he was struck and killed by one of the trains he loved so much. Did he have a heart attack? A stroke? Did it have to do with his high blood pressure? No one knows but his God. We miss you, Uncle George. Whoever left you on that doorstep so many, many years ago, will never know what they had given away!

Here is a little ditty you always used to say. Your daughters do not know if you made it up or if it came from days of yore. I have a feeling, with your wit, that you came up with it all by yourself!

Here's to you as good as you are.
Here's to me as bad as I am.
But as good as you are, and as bad as I am;
I'm as good as you are as bad as I am.

31

KISS & TELL

MY BEST FRIENDS in high school were always boys. I liked spending time with girls, but like I said before, the boys laughed louder. When I was in high school, no one was allowed to touch another human being; only maybe the school nurse. All of our teenage communication had to be done with our eyes and our speech. No talking in the halls between classes. Go to your locker, get your next set of books, and on to the next class. The only chance we had for communication was before school, lunchtime, and after school. Not until my senior year could I actually associate with class members outside of my cousins and kids who went to the same church as we did. My friend, Flossie, had a car, so we tasted freedom for the first time ever! Most of the boys I knew had cars too. After school we would all speed up Oakdale Hill Road until we were out of the city limits. The road was curvy and hilly. The guys drove those roads like race-car drivers. The girls cheered them on. A form of "enlightenment" was upon us (I'm not saying it was from Jesus) as we were every minute about to burst through our skins! I talked and they laughed. I talked some more and they laughed some more. Sometimes a can or two of beer would show up, (stolen that morning from a parent's stash) (Not my house!) and around, the can would be passed; each getting only a couple of sips. What energy had hold of us? Most of us would call it sexual energy. But in our day, kissing was only done in the dark! There was another force pulsing through us. Freedom! Blessed freedom! God watched over us and got most of us through that time. During high school, a girl died from Leukemia in the 11th grade. Our senior yearbook was a tribute to her. During 12th grade, a boy was receiving chemo and radiation for some kind of cancer. I didn't bother to find out what kind because I was immune after soaking in my nine-month cancer bath. I remember him coming back to school with his neck burned bright red. He had fair hair and fair skin so he looked twice as bad. He opened the top of his shirt and showed us some of his chest. Burned to a crisp! He seemed happier than I had ever seen him before. I didn't know then but I know now. I know why now................Anyways, that was thirty-six years ago! They were right on the brink of a cancer cure! Hurray for them! What do I get offered? Chemo and radiation. No thank you. Both children are dead; plus umpteen billion more.

Those few months during the 12th grade that we were lucky enough to experience freedom and be protected by God, were fabulous and few lived. I will never forget the wind in my face, my arm dangling out the window, and the sheer joy of speed! All the time cracking jokes for the boys to find revelry in! Thank you God for watching over us and keeping us safe from ourselves. John was one of the boys either driving or riding in the car. I liked him and he liked me. I could make him laugh easier than any of the other ones. We never dated. There was something invisible between us that would not let us get too close. One time I went over to his house and he was laying on the couch watching TV. We were alone. I sat down on the edge of the couch near the middle of his body. We talked and watched TV. talked and watched TV. "Do you like me?" he asked. "Sure I like you!" I answered. We talked and watched TV, talked and watched TV. "How come you like me?" he asked. "Because you always laugh at my jokes." I answered. "Everyone laughs at you!" he stated. "I know." I said. By then we were smiling at each other. I leaned forward and kissed him on the lips like I would my brother. I backed up and gazed into his eyes, we both started to laugh at the same time. "I guess you're not going to be my girlfriend, are you?" he said. "You never kissed me back!" I screeched. "Yes, I did." He said. "Than no, I'm never going to be your girlfriend!" We laughed and I got up and left.

John is the boy who introduced Nelson and I to each other. He was our best man. I have been digging through old letters and items in my bottom dresser drawer. In there, I found an old school spiral notebook with some vocabulary words in it and various other jottings. On one of the yellowed, wrinkled sheets in the book I found this poem written perhaps during a class or study hall. So here is a day in the life of me, thirty-six years ago.

John is a boy I know
He is everything but slow.
I always have to tell him no;
But all he says is go go go.
He always wants to make a date;
But I have to tell him he's too late.
I'm sure he'd make a very good mate;
But I just can't reciprocate!

Sharon Tuttle Parenteau 12th grade

32

UP, UP, AND AWAY............

From the time I came to terms with the fact that there is no cure for the type of cancer I have, I have tried to embrace my illness as a gift to myself and for others also. I read in a book of a man dying. He was a son, a husband, a father, and a grandfather. The minute I read his words, I was transformed; along with the help of God's grace. This was his goal, as it became mine too. He said, "The best gift I can give my parents, my wife, my children, and their children, is to die with dignity." "I will, in all probability, die before any of them. They are all old enough to know they cannot escape dying either. So as they watch me, they will also be watching the death process itself. I will remain calm, brave, independent, and cheerful as I move forward. I will teach by example, this will be the greatest gift I could ever give them."

At that very instant, I decided to try and do the same. My illness has not been hidden or trivialized by me in any way, shape or form. My mother, as well as my grandchildren, knows that I am moving on into the next part of my life. I do not say I am dying; I say I am moving forward. I am trying my best to continue life as it was before my fortune was told. I continue with knowledge now, knowledge I try to pass on to anyone who has ears… my family and I are fine. We are more than fine; we are alive and living each day with more love and laughter than ever before. We have all been given the gift!

132

Mindette, Nooni, and Gracie gave me a wonderful Christmas gift last year. It is a one-hour flight pass in a glider, purchased at our local small plane airport. Here is the card it was enclosed in.

Mother, you are the love in Christmas

For you, every lesson was taught giving and sharing, not with word, but by constant and beautiful example, thanks, you were and always will be the love in Christmas!

Mindee added: Mom, thank you for your love!

Soar like a bird, feel what it's like to be completely free!

Look at the earth in all its beauty without the hectic ness of the world! We love you, we hope you enjoy your temporary wings!

If I had been wondering if I was doing the right thing, Mindee set my mind at ease that Christmas morning. She and the girls spent Christmas day with Nelson and me. I burnt the meat and tried to "fix" it. It was unfixable. We played out in the snow on Christmas afternoon. We came back in the back door to the kitchen with snow-balls and clumps just clinging to our clothes; covering every inch. "Grandma" threw the first snowball from off my scarf, Mindee the second, Nooni the third and Gracie the fourth. From there on in, it was a free for all. It was delicious fun! It also cleaned the floor better than any cleaner on the market today! Not one of us will ever forget that Christmas afternoon! Especially Grandma. Thank you for making it so easy to be your Mom. It is my pleasure.....

33

POEMS BY BETTY,   MY MOM

Written by Betty
Friday, June 4, 1965

Do you know how it feels to be lonesome,
To face every day feeling blue,
Knowing no one really "needs" you
Or cares a great deal about you?
At meal time you never desire
To partake of the food you prepare
For who can sit and enjoy a meal
When there's nobody there to care?
There's no one to praise or to mock you,
To comfort in times of despair;
You suddenly find you're a lost soul
And happy moments are very rare.
Others look at you and they envy,
They don't know what you're feeling inside,
They only know what they'd like to think-
By no rules must you now abide.
How foolish of them not to wonder
Why your evenings are ever blue,
They can't understand, for you see, Friend

They have never "worn this shoe."
Ask any girl what this feeling
Can do to a life lived like this-
What it means to be searching and reaching
For a true love, for some happiness.
You learn that romance is a storybook theme,
A condition of mind, if you will,
For love-or for a cheap thrill
If you've never known the feeling
Of such utter loneliness,
Find someone who's traveled this road and
Ask in her moment of weakness.
She'll admit that it's not all as "rosy"
As to others it may appear
For she knows what's on the minds of men
When she passes and their looks turn to leers.
Guys think a gal in a spot like this
Need their attention and tenderness
But they forget that she has feelings too,
And will give much more than she gets.
So you think that a girl who is footloose
Is as happy as she can be
And you envy her when you see how
She "appears" to bc truly free.
There is no such thing as freedom,
Though others may not agree,
There is only heartbreak and loneliness
Look around and I'm sure you will see.
The years take toll on all of us
And soon, before even you know
You find that life has passed you by
And you've nothing left to show.
You search back through a memories book
Try to relive past happy times

But you find only faded photos there
And how your face has taken on lines.
You're older now, and you're wiser too
You can see past mistakes you've made
But there's no going back so you must accept
That the price for a "free" life is paid.
So take my advice and don't envy
The gal who "seems" fancy free,
For she's looking at you and wishing
That the gal in your life were she.

Written for Carl's mom- 1970
By Betty

The Lord walks beside us each step of the way,
    To comfort and guide us throughout every day.
We know of His presence, we feel He is near-
    How else could we walk through life without fear.

Through trials He comforts; he eases our pain,
    We know that love given is never in vain.
He strengthens and guides us through life's rough pathway
    That our footsteps not falter, from the path we'll not stray.

How precious this gift given us by God-
    His Son's blessed presence as through life we trod.
For what is asked of us by the Father above
    But to receive His blessings and give others our love.

Then, as our life's journey comes near to the end,
    We value the closeness of such a dear friend,
And though through the valley of the shadow of death we trod,
    There's a lightness of heart-for we shall see God.

POEM BY BETTY

Excuse me, please, may I come in
   And interrupt your day?
I promise I won't stay too long,
   Then I'll be on my way.

I will not try to tell you
   All that's in my heart today;
I failed-but it was not my job
   So I'll just walk away.

We cannot know the future
   And what is past is gone,
I wanted things the way they were
   But life kept moving on.

I didn't feel I'd hoped for much,
   I wanted nothing more
Than to hold us all together
   The siblings numbering four.

I know the years can take their toll
   We're busy as can be,
I'd only hoped we'd find the time
   To stay a "family".

9/24/93

Hold on to Today

As life goes on and time flies by
  There's barely time to say
A message I would like to leave-
  Just hold on to today.

The yesterdays are all said and done,
  No need to wish they'd stay,
What's done is done-we must go on
  And hold on to today.

A word we spoke in anger,
  A deed we left undone,
A hand not yet extended-
  A song still left unsung.

When we wake up each morning,
  It's now a brand new day;
Too late to change our yesterday-
  So hold on to today.

A smile comes very easy,
  A kind word we can say,
A loving hand extended
  Helps us hold on to today.

The memories shall linger,
  They will never go away;
They make it so much easier
  To hold on to today.

You ask-"What about tomorrow?"
  It doesn't matter anyway-

Remember, when tomorrow comes-
That it will be "today."

Betty   11/14/92

I Will Smile When All Around Me

I will smile when all around me
  Seems to crumble and to fall,
I'll start out every morning-head held
  High and walking tall.
I'll not let those around me try to
  Break my spirits down,
Nor will I let them dash my hopes
  Into the ground.

I'll set my plans and goals in life,
  I'll know what I can do-
And if I really work at it,
  I'm sure I'll see them through.

How many times we've heard it said-
  "My plans have always failed"
when actually, if truth be known,
  no plans at all availed.

Life goes on-despite it all,
  It does not wait for us,
We cannot try to shift the blame
  When life turns out a "bust".

So kick up your heels and forge ahead-
  Life's not so bad, you see-
We make it what it is-they say
  But you can't prove that by me.

   Betty   3/17/93

34

LETTER FOR ALL FROM MANLEY JR. MY DAD

My father, Right after his death, sent to a psychic friend to share with all. For those of you who do not know me... I am the person who was granted the joy of sharing these last six months of Manley's bodily life. I have been asked to speak to you today-not only to share my knowledge of this great man, but also to enable me to break the tie and let him go. Manley Elias, the truest man of God who I have ever known, was my teacher...and it was with these past six months spent with me that his mission on earth was completed and his spirit was able to loose itself from it's bodily encasement and join the infinite perfect ness of God.

Our relationship was utterly unique. During these six months we had developed a "knowing" that takes most couples 50 years. Manley Elias was the love of my life and he developed wholeness within me...enough to sustain me for all the days to come. He was my teacher, my playmate, he was my best friend, and he was my love.

A multi-talented man...I must say that first and foremost, because of his love for God, Manley was an ordained Methodist minister. Very early in his ministry he felt compelled to leave and search out truths...for he had come to understand that with God-there are no limits. God embraces not only the Christian-but also the Jew, the Moslem, the Buddhist-right down the line to the illiterate natives of the jungle.

Manley was one of the greatest teachers I have ever experienced. He was a philosopher, a psychologist, one "hell of a" great cook, as he would say, "really I'm the best there is in the Triple Cities." His interests were endless-books and learning were a passion, he loved the theater, movies, the opera, jazz. He loved to dance and sing. Manley loved life. He loved people. He was the "truest friend" a person could have—if anyone decided to be that close to him. You had to pursue him---he would not pursue you.

The workings of his mind constantly amazed me…for he had a photographic memory. A wealth of information was stored between those two beautiful ears of his…and he could refer back to any topic he wanted at any given time.

I must refer to a recent incident with one of his young close friends, Jeff. During the course of their conversation Manley said, "Hey, this body of mine is getting old." Jeff replied, "Manley, you are the youngest old person I know." So true. Although the body he inhabited was indeed growing tired-his mind remained young and adventurous and his "spirit" free and unattached.

I am a full-time student at SUNY Binghamton in the fine arts department. All this week during spring break, Manley was in the sculpture foundry with me (my apprentice) helping me to beat "old father time" to get some pieces ready which needed to be photo-graphed—a process necessary in the "art world" in order to qualify for certain exhibitions. He loved "learning" no matter what the sub-ject matter. For Manley there were no closed doors. Two weeks ago, Manley helped take some of the pressure off me at the universi-ty by writing a history paper that was due for midterms. "Don't tell the professor on me." I said. Manley's answer was, "You know the material anyway." It was his suggestion to help and I sensed his en-thusiasm. My joy existed within his, and so I said, "Sure, terrific!" All this past week, Manley kept saying, "I can't wait until I see what mark I got on your paper, Darling." At this present time, Manley knows what the mark is, but I do not. (He died before I got it back.)

Manley dearly loved his family. He dearly loved his life as a young boy growing up. To his mother he wants to say, "Mom, you were the best mother any child could ask for. Remember, Mom, how everyone took turns reading stories to us kids. How proud I was when it was your turn."

To his father he wants to say, "I am so happy that we were not only father and son but I am thrilled that we also became such good friends. Do not be sad. I am very happy today, Easter Sunday (my favorite holiday) in spirit. Mom, Dad, you gave me the stability, the strength, the guidance that was necessary for me to grow and fulfill my purpose in life."

To Cork, my eldest son; "How often I seem to think of the early days, Cork, in the ministry. The structure that your mom and I lived in was frequently so cold and I would cradle you on my chest-in bed with us-in order to keep you warm. And to think that you grew into such a good friend of mine---another rare combination indeed."

To Sharon….my eldest daughter… "Honey, you are the "apple of my eye".. my little "pink bundle." Thank you for all those "little things," your femininity, your charm. Give Cork a hug for me and know that I am always going to be around you both.

To my son, Scott, "I truly did the best I could, Scott. Take strength and do what should be done. It is time now, time to put the childish things away and to grow in wisdom. I truly love you, Scott."

To my daughter, Amy, "I have truly missed you. I wish that your mother and I could have stayed together so that I could have enjoyed teaching you and the watching of your 'growing up years'".

To all my grandchildren, I send my greatest love and hope that your "growing up years" and pursuits in life will be filled with happiness, and "knowing" within the Godhead.

To my wives, the women in my life, I say "I loved you all, as I still do now. I never, never started a relationship with any other intention then it would last the rest of our lives."

To my friend, Jeff, I send an apology, "Well, I know we had great plans for this new business venture we were about to embark upon, but it was destiny that I was called away to a better area of employment. Don't fret, let it pass. You, my buddy, are going to do just fine."

To his friends who loved him, he returns the same.

To his friends who love him…he returns the same.

To the members of the Masons of which he was a member, Manley says, "Thank you. I truly found great joy in being a Mason. I would have found great satisfaction if it had been possible for me to be more active. And you know, really, I just loved being a Shiners Clown."

The tears we have been shedding these past few days…we must realize…are not for him…but for ourselves because we have lost bodily contact with him. Do not be sad. Sometime ago, before I knew him-Manley had found the truths within God that he had been seeking. He didn't believe these truths to be true. He KNEW these to be true. During meditation, his spirit was capable of leaving his body and looking at himself. Elias stated on many occasions, "I am ready to pass out of my body anytime now. I don't just believe…I know what God's truths are.."

With this in mind, let us all join together in joyfulness and praise that the "light of God" within Manley Jr., his spirit, is now free to roam and assist us through his influence for the greater glory of God-always.

35

LETTERS FOR SHARON

Dear Mom,   1998

I sat down intending to write some beautiful, poetic letter; sounding as if it came from a published work of art. I realized I am not poetic nor a published writer. I am just someone who knows how they're feeling, but can't find an eloquent way to say it.

You are my mother; I am your daughter. When our souls were matched in the heavens, someone was having a good day! We're so much alike as we are different.

You are my role model when it comes to mothering. If I'm in a spot where I don't know what to do-I stop and wonder how you would handle the situation. Always the main point is to surround them with my love as I have been surrounded.

I know you are my kindred spirit, my best friend and female soul mate. What my world would be without you, I cannot comprehend.

I see myself eighty years old and sitting, looking out my window, still with my memories of my mother to bring a smile. That cinnamon-sugar toast. Those days and nights of endless laughter where one of us was either going to pee our pants or throw up!

Through all the good times and bad-you are always there.

Thank you Mom, for being the true thing and for holding my hand through my life together with you.

Thank you, Lord, for sending me to my mom.

Love always,

Mindee

Dearest Sharon,

August 20, 2003

Where do I start? It isn't easy to put some words on paper since we talk everyday on the phone. First, I guess I'd say thanks for calling me every day. It means a lot to know you care, and it gives me a chance to say I care and love you. Many times I've told you how very proud I am of you, but I can never say it enough.

You were so right when you said family is important to me. I should add here my thanks to you for the little extra push to get me to write my brother after more than five years of no contact with him. I knew it was up to me to do that, I just kept putting it off.

So many things you say and do amaze me, such as your wisdom and knowledge of a wide world of subjects. I'm not sure why because the Bible tells us " and a little child shall lead them." And you will always be my little girl. You and your brother are always in my thoughts and prayers. I'm so proud of both of you. If only I could take on all of your worries and cares and health problems. I know that this is not possible; it is not in God's plan for us, but if I could you know I would! I love you both so much.

Do you remember several years ago when you sent me a card every day for a week before my birthday? There was one verse that I memorized and it has stayed with me all these years. Here it is:

First we creep, then we walk

Eventually we learn to talk

As time goes by, we start to stoop

Getting old is pigeon poop.

Not a day goes by that I don't repeat the last line many times.

I hope you will realize that I am behind you in your endeavors. I know I have not been a model mother, but I thank God for the chance to do better in whatever time each of us may have left. Your two daughters and granddaughters are your life now, and I'm sure that all you do for them and the time spent with them will be forever cherished by them. You've done a good job and I'm so proud of you and I love you very much.

All my love,

Your Mom.

Dearest Daughter,

You asked during a time of contemplation if your father could only write you a letter now, for your second book. Well here it is! And two days early from the due date you requested! "Seek and ye shall find; ask and it shall be given unto you."

When I ascended to the new dimension, I was soon to find out you would soon (in our time) be following. This news made my soul soar even higher! I am pleased with your progress into the next dimension. The Master and I will continue to guide you along.

As you know, your cancer is the best offered in the universe! Undoubtedly, you have noticed few discomforts along with a great awakening! This, my dear one, is truly a gift from God. He is shining on you continually; I am making sure of that! As soon as the peace was granted, I knew you would let God's light come through you as an inspiration to others. I promise you, you will not suffer; you will rise unencumbered faster than the speed of sound.

I will be first in line to greet you, my dear daughter ; as I have been anticipating our meeting since my arrival. Everyone will be there; all you have requested. Along with your past ancestry, you will meet Patsy, Marilyn, Buddy, Judy, Dean, Frank, everyone who has ever crossed your mind! We all await your crossover! Fear not, for I am with you always, God said, and so am I.

As you may or may not know, I studied with Mahirashi back in the 1970's. He taught me transcendental meditation. During that time, I found it opening up the gospel and convincing me as to why I could never give up the Christ in all those years of not to Christ like living. I found immortality and such a love. The "I am" that was before Abraham was; "is" and "that" dwells in me and "I" in "it".

The way one lives his life is what counts. Man is a free agent under God. Each day all of you will be saved by something, through seeing the truth, of which many may perhaps qualify just the day before. Salvation is a growing thing. There is no valid "experience" except life and how it teaches us God's will and purpose for us. Look for no second coming of Christ except as He comes into the hearts of those who open up to Him. This is the reality. Don't sit on your hands and wait for some kingdom, for one can see the Life of Christ in the lives of others and this does much more for the advancement of our kingdom. Interpret the Bible in the light of science and history. It is inspired, but so are a lot of other writings about God. Man experiences God in one-way or another and sets down his feelings. When "truth" is spoken, it is "the word of God". In your Bible, you will find in the Old Testament, where Joshua told the children of Israel to kill all the men, women, and children in the Promised Land and this was commanded in the name of God. You must certainly see this is not the same concept of the God of Love of which Christ spoke. "If your enemy strikes you on the right cheek, turn to him the left also." And again; "love your enemies, do good to them that despitefully use you." Some of the Bible is mythology. It still amazes me that people can accept Greek cultural myth and Roman myth, but are unwilling to think the Hebrews had a mythology! Why should they be any different from any other culture? It is true that God chose to reveal Himself more perfectly to them and subsequently to the followers of the Christ, but all men start primitively.

So often in churches we see not the spirit of Christ, but rather the spirit of evil (what people call Satan or the devil) the world has had many anti-Christ's. They, some serving in churches, no more ex-

148

emplify the spirit of the Christ than Hitler or any of the false God's did. Their policy of separation is directly contrary to the true word of God (Christ). Our righteousness is as filthy rags in the sight of God. Self is the real devil. Self-centeredness is the one thing that holds us back.

As you daily die to the old, natural self, your Christhood grows. Empty yourself daily of self, and God will fill you more and more. The kingdom will come for you. You will be liberated, free, free of birth, death, the rebirth cycle. The kingdom is "within" and you will "know" that it is true. Your mind (soul) will be one with God. "I and the Father are one."

Give my love to all! Keep building God's kingdom with your light. I have written everything out of my love for you. Bless you, my daughter, I send you my love daily, and wait with eagerness to see you and your family again.

Yours in oneness,

Dad

(This letter was sent to me, on an impulse, from out of the blue by a distant, distant cousin after going through old papers. My father wrote it in 1956. I was six years old.)

26

LITTLE SQUIRT

The year is 2003. As I drive the roads and highways, people are obliged to pull off the road and talk on their cell phones. How did we all survive so long in our cars, not bring able to communicate with others? I don't have a cell phone; I am pulling off the road to grab a pen and notepad to write down my thoughts, as I am sure I could not possibly remember them the ten minutes it will take me to arrive home.

I desperately need to record everything that shadows my mind. It is all so profound to me. These revelations just astound. Much of this will mean nothing to most. Something is compelling me, enticing me, not to let one drop of this free from its destiny; that being to be shared.

Can you find a story about a daughter, a father, and a lemon so intriguing that you must read on. So simple, so easy, so unnatural. My first book refers back to several summer visits with my father. Another recollection is finding myself in the kitchen with my dad. The conversation was exciting and lively. He knew no other kind. He was glad I was there; I could feel it! I was glad I was there; he could feel it! As he chattered and sliced into a lemon for one of his famous dishes, he paused. His faced brightened as he dropped the lemon on the counter and smelled his fingers. "Sis, have you ever in your entire life seen or smelled anything like this?" He asked as he shoved his fingers under my nose. He didn't wait for an answer. He picked up the lemon, he smelled it and touched his tongue to its flesh.

"Look at this color! Have you ever in your whole life seem anything like this color?" He never waited for my answer. He stuck a half of lemon in my face and told me to taste it. "Dad, I know what a lemon tastes like!" "No, I mean really taste it, don't just say you do."

I laughed and stuck out my tongue a little and he touched the lemon to it. His face was absolutely lit and he was glowing as he enjoyed this simple lemon. It is the simple things we remember. To this day, I cannot see, smell, or taste a lemon without thinking of my father and that night his face shone!

Recently, Nooni and I were cutting lemon for a fish dinner we were preparing. "Nooni, look at this lemon, have you ever seen anything like it in your life?" "Oh, Grandma, it's just a lemon." She said. "Just a lemon, Nooni, smell this right now!" I said as I stuck it under her nose. "Grandma, you got it up my nose and it burns!" She shouted. "Oh, I'm sorry. Let Grandma get you a wet cloth to wipe it off." I never asked her to taste it, although she did squirt a little on her haddock. I have proved it over and over, time and time again; there is, and only will be, one Manley Elias Tuttle, Jr.

I love you, Dad!

27

SOOOOO   WHAAATTTT!!!!!!!

I FIND IT BOTH fitting and apropos to end this part of my life as it began. It didn't begin with me or my father or his father or his father. It is staggering to add up the members of your ancestry. To think it all started with two young children; born, meeting, and starting a life together.

The stories I know, only go back as far as my grandfather. He and his sister and brothers used to dress for school in front of the only source of heat for their house: a potbelly stove. Each one burned their butt trying to get as close to it as possible. I know his mother was an angel of a person. He only had good things to say about her and her mother, his grandma. I know his mother made his father remove all the marble tops from all the tables in their house and had them replaced with wood. My grandfather, in his '80's, was still wondering if those marble tabletops were still out behind the shed. He just knew their value would be astronomical. I know in the winter they all shared the same bath water on Saturday night. In the summer, swimming took care of their hygiene. I know they ate what they grew and wore clothes their mother made. Most were hand-me-downs for him. I know they went to church every week. In the summer, all the boys rode horses and tied them out front. So I now know their horses also went to church. I know in the winter, "thunder pots" were used during the night, pulled out from under their beds, each getting their turn to empty them in the outhouse the next morning. I know my grandfather walked two miles to school and home again....both ways were up hill......with bare feet....... in the winter.......and he was grateful to be able to do it! I wish I had asked more questions. He was forever eager to talk of his past. I wish I asked more important questions of him. My grandmother was the first to tell me the story of Stonewall Jackson and Blue Dress Alice. Her version was a much gentler one than his. To hear his version told in front of my grandmother was surely a keeper. "You and Verna and Charlotte, all boy crazy! Did you really think we didn't know what all of you were thinking? You weren't the first one to have eyes for Stonewall you know, I practically had to beat them all off with a stick!" he roared. "Oh, you just stop that right now! What do you want her to think!" Grandma delighted, as she realized she had won the heart of Stonewall Jackson back in 1918.

That was the day my grandfather, as a ten-year old boy, proclaimed, SOOOO WHAAAT! I ponder these 2 words everyday now. They have a secret meaning hidden deep within.

I had a dream not too long after I became "accustomed" to my invader. (cancer) and my fate. My grandfather and my cat Riley, who is now fifteen-years old, were walking down a grassy knoll, side by side, toward me as I stood looking up from the bottom. Riley has never been allowed outside to roam since he was a kitten. I found him too close to the road one day and his wanderings were immediately over.

As I stood at the base of the hill and realized it really was the two of them descending, I hollered out, "Grandpa, we don't let Riley outside!" I was nervous and agitated to think he was so careless with my sweet cat. He chuckled as they drew nearer and said, "Oh, he's all right! He's having fun!" "But Grandpa, he's not used to going outside, he'll run off!" "Oh, he wandered off from the apple orchard for a little while, but he came back!" (We were shouting to each other as we were still a distance apart.) "What were you doing in the apple orchard?" I asked. "Having a picnic!" he proclaimed. "With

153

who?" I asked. "Everybody!" he said, as he opened his arms wide and laughed. By then he was by my side. "Grandpa, please don't take Riley outside again, he'll get hit by a car, stolen, or he'll run away, so please......Grandpa was laughing at me so hard he could barely answer. "There are no cars. There is no one to steal him and where would he run away to?" My grandfather had been dead several years when I had this dream. Riley and I are still on planet earth. But before I woke, I realized I was either having a dream or experiencing some time and place in the future. It was grand to see my grandfather again. He was smiling, tan, and had a stomach full of picnic food; three of his favorite things. That morning and all day long, a song would not leave my mind.... "Don't sit under the apple tree, with anyone else but me, no, no, no, anyone else but me, no, no, no, till I come marching home.........

So I began with a "SOOOO WHHAATTT" all those many years ago, and I want to end with a "SOOOOO WHHAATTTT." So what if I did everything wrong.....so what if I did everything right? I'm still in the same boat. So what if I didn't care enough....so what if I cared too much......I'm still in the same boat; so what a lot of things. In the grand picture, does any of it really matter? Was it all mapped out before any of us ever came here? As children and as adults, there is no one in this whole world, backwoods excluded, that does not know and sing the "Row, row, row, your boat" song. As Nooni and I tried to sing it one day in staggered harmony, we just ended up laughing. Then all of a sudden the words struck me with such sharpness that I had to reel back and I dropped silent. "What's wrong Grandma? Why aren't you trying to sing?" she asked as she giggled because one of us or the other would wind up "falling into" the others song.

"I'm thinking, Nooni, I'm thinking.....let Grandma sing this one time by herself, ok?" "Ok Grandma, go ahead." In my best singing voice, no clowning around, I began the song slow and deliberate. "Row, row, row your boat, gently down the stream. Merrily, merrily, merrily, life....is.....but......but a dream.......a dream......a dream?

SSOOOOOOOOOOOOOO Grandpa, WHAAAAAAAAT have you been up to?" Could a childhood song, written haphazardly hundreds of years ago by who knows who, hold the secret to reality? Have we all had it shoved under our noses at home, school, and at play and eluded the meaning for all these hundreds of years? I know the truth is something simple, too simple to ever enter our minds. When we receive the realization, we will all roar with laughter. It will be a merry time!

Remember teaching me the song "I like to go swimmin' with bowlegged women and swim between their legs!" one day when we were in the river and Grandma got so mad at you!?"

OBITUARY

I, Sharon Parenteau, of Endicott, NY, formerly Sharon Tuttle, of Johnson City, NY have gone to my glory on age. For some time now, I have been a student of life, with cancer as my teacher. I hope I was as good a student as it was a teacher. My brother, Cork, you were right. It truly was a gift. I wouldn't have traded places with anyone. Nelson, my husband and life partner, I love you so much! I wait for you in angel wings! Someday to see our two loving daughters surrounded by the light of God will fill my soul with joy! Nicelee Fall Hollenback, I love you! Mindette Marcelle Parenteau, I love you! Mindee, you gave me the greatest gift that can be given, you are the wonderful mother of my two granddaughters: Sara Emilee and Grace Caroline. Grandma is your special angel now. Remember I am just a zipper away. Step inside and I will be there to help you. You are Grandma's babies. You will continue to fill my heart with joy! My brother, (Cork) Manley Elias Tuttle III, great admirer of the written word; you read the Bible from front

155

to back when you were only eight years old. Thank you for all the books passed down. Now do this for me...write your book, it will be a best seller! Years ago, as children, you once said you never wanted to be separated from me. I'll never forget that. And I promise you now, that I will never leave you. I love you, my brother. My mother and friend, my patient listener, I love you so much! You have been my rock throughout this whole journey. I will be first in line to greet you. My baby brother and baby sister, Scott and Amy, I love you. You will be forever young in my heart! I will remember all my aunts and uncles, both passed and present, for their love and guidance as I grew. Thank you all for your love! I will remember my many cousins with whom I grew up with, both passed and present. I'll never forget the fun we had! I love you all! Our cats, their love has filled our home with laughter for many years! I love you all! Special love to Riley James, our oldest cat, who kept me company, right by my side, the minute I got into bed! Our two min pins- Penny and Mikey; I am so in love with you both. Thanks for all the fun and laughter Everyone who reads this; please go to my employer, Miracle Ear at Sears, and remember me to Shane. No finer family or business owners you will ever find! Truly good, honest people! It was my pleasure and privilege to be a part of your company. I thank you all for your honest concern and encouragement. My father, The Reverend Manley Elias Tuttle Jr., loved the Lord with every inch of his soul. He shone with the light of God! He went home at age 58; leaving his body to science. In memory of him and to honor my grandchildren, I do the same. My last gift to mankind! There will be a celebration of life in our home to be announced at a later date. Please send remembrances of me to Westover United Methodist Church. Johnson City, N.Y. Members both passed and present, among them my grandparents who raised me, Manley and Alice Tuttle Sr., are responsible for the peace and power from God that got me to this place joyously! From the bottom of my heart and in the face of God I say I love you and I thank you. Thanks again to everyone who crossed my path! It was a blast! As my oldest granddaughter would say, "Grandma, you're up, up, and away!"

Written in 2002

PEARLY GATES

Conversation between God and Sharon at the Pearly Gates

Hi.
Hi.
Who are you?
I seem to be Light.
Where did you come from?
Nowhere and everywhere.
What brought you here?
Faith.
What will keep you here?
Hope.
How old are you?
Ageless.
What do you know?
Everything and nothing.
What do you believe?
Truth.
Where are you going?
Everywhere...never ending.
What do you seek?
Knowledge.
What do you like to do?

Look up.
What makes you happy?
Wisdom.
What have people forgotten?
The laws of nature cannot be broken.
What does the world need most?
Stillness.
What is your favorite color?
White.
Is white a color?
White is every color.
What is time?
What is time?
What are your expectations of Heaven?
Boundless.
What is your name?
I am that I am.
Hey, me too!…..Now, God,……. do you have any questions
for me?

By Sharon Parenteau   November 21, 2001

CONCLUSION

Utter no sigh of agony, but draw upon my face with your finger
The symbol of love and joy....

Mourn me not with apparel of black, but dress in color and rejoice
(with me).......

Leave me then; leave me and depart on mute feet.....
Leave this place that which death hast let you visit because of
me.

Go now, back to your earthly world......
Leave me......

Unknown Author

And when her work was done, she laughed in the forest.

Forget not that the earth delights to feel your bare feet and the
winds long to play with your hair.
Kahlil Gibran 1923

And when the shadow fades and is no more, the light that lingers becomes a shadow to another light.

I come from elsewhere, and though I do not know where that is, I am certain to return there in the end.

When I die
I will soar with angels,
And when I die to the angels,
What I shall become
You cannot imagine.

Author Unknown

To Contact the Author

By Mail:
Sharon Parenteau
P.O. Box 5699
Endicott N.Y. 13763
U.S.A.

or E-Mail her at:
icryforthelittlegirl@earthlink.net